NO LAUGHING MATTER

NO LAUGHING MATTER

Norman Hudis

APEX PUBLISHING LTD

First published in 2008 by
Apex Publishing Ltd
PO Box 7086, Clacton on Sea, Essex, CO15 5WN

www.apexpublishing.co.uk

Copyright © 2008 by Norman Hudis
The author has asserted his moral rights

British Library Cataloguing-in-Publication Data
A catalogue record for this book
is available from the British Library

ISBN 1-906358-15-X   978-1-906358-15-0

Typeset in 12.5pt Baskerville Win95BT

Production Manager: Chris Cowlin

Cover Design: Siobhan Smith

Printed and bound in Great Britain

To Rita,
without whom,
nothing

FOREWORD
By Peter Rogers

Norman Hudis has been such a part of my life that it is difficult for me to stand aside and talk about him.

I knew him first as a film publicist when I was a scriptwriter. He always struck me as a no-nonsense character and I would not have imagined in those days that he was particularly endowed with a sense of humour. Though, come to think of it, anyone who indulges in film publicity must have a sense of humour somewhere.

However, Norman gave up film publicity to become a scriptwriter. I, for one, am glad that he did. Another producer gave him a three-year contract but was unable to make use of him, or, should I say, could not make use of his talents. When that producer told me of his problems I offered to take over the contract and so began a very successful series of comedy films. In my opinion Norman could write anything, but we began with a comedy which was so successful that it seemed a pity not to continue.

Considering the tight censorship of those days it's a wonder that anybody could write a comedy at all apart from fat-headed farce.

I particularly told Norman that I wanted a laugh and

tear-jerk script and that is what I got - one after another. Bless him.

Curiously enough, when Norman left me to go to America and other writers took over, none of them was able to do the tear-jerk.

I know that Norman has gone from strength to strength in his new environment and rightly so.

I have nothing but happy memories of our association and a relationship that no others have achieved.

He's a bloody good scriptwriter, if you ask me.

Peter Rogers

CONTENTS

TO BEGIN IN THE MIDDLE:

THE CARRY ONS

Good Evening - Great Day!

7 May 2006. The car halted at the Victory Club, Seymour Street, Marble Arch, London, favoured lodging for Rita and me when in England.

We were on our way to Pinewood Studios, Iver Heath, Buckinghamshire - concluding our 6,000+ mile journey from California for *An Evening With* ... well, me - organized by the energetic Carry On historian, Morris Bright.

No false modesty, but I was truly more than a touch surprised that hundreds of fiercely dedicated Carry On aficionados showed up to meet, in the studio's oak-panelled dining room, the writer of the first six movies in that series.

Here's the report I supplied to George Seaton's Carry On website (**www.carryonline.com**), which attracts thousands of hits weekly:

The jollity began with the screening of the trailers of my six Carry Ons, followed by short scenes from some of them. Since these consisted mostly of people falling down, I was relieved that a further set of clips indicated satisfactorily that I was also capable of writing dialogue. Especially

3

touching in this connection were excerpts from No Kidding *and* Twice Round the Daffodils.

The untiring Carry-On-ers then sought autographs. Though they clearly wanted Rita's too, she modestly declined to sit beside me. The people sought her out just the same, as the original 'Nurse', and because of her additional medical association with showbiz as Technical Adviser on Nursing for the last two seasons of MASH *in Hollywood.*

A fragile, youngish man told me: "Your films saved my life."

He had suffered a near-terminal sickness and, during long, painful hospitalization, had repeatedly viewed cassettes of my films as well as seeing them on TV. They cheered him up sufficiently to cause him to make the emotional claim quoted above.

Of course they did not 'save his life': doctors/nurses/his own will achieved his survival, but that laughter is a good auxiliary medicine is not, I think, to be denied. It was lump-in-the-throat time for me during the couple of minutes we spent together. Only once before has anything I wrote (a 'Marcus Welby' - see 'From Pine to Holly' later) done any good to a viewer beyond mere entertainment.

The other end of the scale was sheer hilarity: a jolly, buxom lady who assured Rita that her difficulty in breast-feeding was solved when she laughed so heartily at Teacher *on TV, while trying to feed baby, that the resulting muscular convulsions expressed her milk.*

Morris briefly interviewed me and then the evening was thrown open to questions.

Maybe I was getting a little light-headed by now, but when asked what historical character I would have liked to take the lead in a C/On, all that sprang to mind was Macbeth. I wanted to elaborate and add that it would have been fun for Hattie Jacques to play all three witches, magically rolled into one, if only to save on casting. This would keep up two reputations: the series' for inexpensive production; and her good humour about her figure, but the next question, whatever it was, came fast and the moment passed.

To tie this off, because it's not included in the website report:

It was only while writing this book that I learned, from Hattie's 2007 biography, that, after a while, she did say that she was tiring of 'the fat stuff' in scripts.

But she never raised such an objection when working with me. To which I can only say, bypassing the usual casual inflection of the phrase, "Bless her", for being, as one viewer wrote in, a "good sport" in this connection, on the one occasion when I focused principally on her physique.

This was in the TV series *Our House*, and the story stemmed entirely from her character wanting to lose weight. She said to me:

"All that matters, dear, is that it's funny and good-natured."

I did not embarrass her by commenting that those words defined her.

The episode 'A Thin Time' is, incidentally, the only tape out of my shows in that series that, as far as I know, is held in the archives of the National Film Theatre; and master writer Eric Sykes thrilled me by telling Hattie that it was "a classic". The remaining tapes of the first season seem to have been wiped.

Back to the website report:

What advice, I was asked, would I give to anyone who wanted to be a screenwriter?

*On the way back to the hotel I thought of the most practical one: marry money. At the time, however, I stated my old-fashioned belief that you have to **want** to write, so insistently, that you seek very little or no formal tuition but, like thousands before you, should find out how to do it reasonably right by doing it dead wrong first and hacking your own path through the jungle of art, technique and commerce. Very old-curmudgeon of me, no doubt, but, being given a certificate by a college, doth not a writer make, in this grumpy scribe's opinion.*

Questioned as to why the first version of Carry On Again Nurse, *mine, for which producer Peter Rogers brought me back from Hollywood for a few weeks, was not produced, I launched into:*

"The powers-that-be - now the unlamented powers-that-were - decreed that the budget of £1,500,000 was excessive for such a parochial subject. This prudent decision did not prevent them from backing such parochial British films as Four Weddings and a Funeral, Lock, Stock and Two Smoking Barrels *and* The Long Good Friday, *all of which fared well outside Britain. Far less profitably, they lavished money on intense, introspective movies about*

intellectuals practising joyless adultery in Hampstead, sometimes innovatively telling these stories backwards. To turn down our film, they were, in my view, plainly and obtusely wrong."

This earned the most sustained applause of the evening, which shook even me. I like to think that at least some of the C/On supporters present had read my Again Nurse script in Morris Bright and Robert Ross' book The Lost Carry Ons and found it, as I do, probably the most inventive, affectionate and well-placed C/On ever. And it would have provided fitting, final, and thoroughly characteristic appearances of the entire regular cast. Peter Rogers, not so incidentally, agrees.

One should not let things rankle, but I'm only human and this unjust and exasperating experience remains a J. Arthur Rankler.

Peter Rogers appeared for the final part of the evening and would not take his place beside me until he had located and embraced a further embarrassed Rita.

Our bantering time together passed amusingly: I acknowledged him as a producer of insight and determination; he went overboard and described me as a *genius. He declared he missed me and always wondered why I went to America, to which I replied, because they asked me and paid me.*

His reply was as adroit as ever: "We all make mistakes," implying that my mistake was in leaving and his was for letting me leave. Analysis of these opinions must await another time. Meanwhile, he presented me with a new portrait of the original Carry On cast and the evening quietly faded into memory.

Those in attendance included: my London associates film producer Steve Walsh; theatrical entrepreneur Marc Sinden (Peter Rogers' godson); composers Gwyn and Jane Arch; and my British agent Janet Glass.

And, almost all of Rita's family - a warm reminder that the days we spent in London on this memorable trip also encompassed our Golden Wedding anniversary.

Men Carrying On!

It is fitting and convenient, here, right up front, to recall an equally exhilarating Carry On Evening with me, thanks to the tireless Carry On chronicler Robert Ross. Engaged to deliver a sold-out lecture at the

National Film Theatre, he heard I was in London and at once handed the evening over to me, for my memories and a frank Q&A with the audience.

A rather uneasy consequence: after the talk, a young man approached me to say that he had almost given up trying to be a writer, but my talk etc., encouraged him to continue his efforts. If he sees this, maybe he'll get in touch and let me know if my inspiration proved to be fruitful or disastrous ...

Tucked away in the mountainous lore of the Carry Ons, is the probably not very well-known fact that Robert Ross gained his B.A. with Honours degree from the University of North London for his dissertation on "Male Sexuality In The Carry Ons".

You will not find me lacking in comment on almost any topic in these pages - but this one, I confess, leaves me silent and awed.

Just as intriguing, I think, is that the above-mentioned Morris Bright, as well as continuing his Carry On interest (and Biz-writing generally, notably definitive histories of both Pinewood and Shepperton Studios), is the Leader of Hertsmere Borough Council, which owns world-famous Elstree Studios and is determined to keep it functioning.

Back now to Pinewood, which consumed many of my English working years, long before the Carry Ons stratospherically topped them all. So it's only fair to report, briefly, on how I wound up there.

After stints in publicity in London, and at Islington and Denham Studios (both long since closed), I went on to Pinewood and spent my final seven years in that activity there.

Moving On

Thence came the dawn of me as a full-time writer.

I'd had a stage play, *Here is the News*, produced in repertory to not bad reviews. Executive Producer Earl St John took me out of publicity and gave me a modest screenwriting contract. I'll recall this colourful character in a little more detail later.

Two years of enthusiastic but unfilmed scripting and off I went into freelancing, scripting about twenty or so "B" features.

The Americans paid the stars and got the rights of the

films in the Western hemisphere; a British company made the film, usually a hearty thriller, in three weeks tops; and television wiped out the B-feature industry in not much more time than that.

One such script of mine did not fit the pattern, and did without American involvement. This was the unexpected million-pound box-office success *The Tommy Steele Story* for Peter Rogers at Beaconsfield Studios. We went on to another Steele musical, my first film with director Gerald Thomas, by which time I was under contract to Peter Rogers Productions Limited.

For the next six years Peter and Gerry loomed largest in my writing life and became, in my mind, the indissoluble pairing I will refer to as P-G, not failing to point out that this stood also for 'Please God'.

Then, the Carry Ons ...

... and the story of how they came about has been told many times over the past 50 years, in wild variation and unexpected places. Can I ever forget the American club theatre owner, deep in the heart of California's San Fernando Valley, who told me to my face that he had "directed all the Carry Ons"?. I will not sully these memories with obscenity and blasphemy but, at the time, I had no hesitation in employing both to his jaw-dropping face.

I will quote, here, in this connection, the cautionary old saw:

"Success has many fathers. Failure is an orphan."

Further, let it simply be said that, for Peter Rogers and Gerald Thomas, I scripted the first six and wallowed in the instant riotous success, and all it brought me, all around the world. Still something of an American record, I believe, for a very Brit comedy, *Nurse* ran for a year at the Crest Theatre in Westwood, Los Angeles.

Enough of that. Let's settle for the accolade of Karen Pedersen, Library Director of the Writers' Guild of America (West). She has declared that the Carry Ons have "gone beyond mere Cult into the realm of full blown Phenomenon".

My major contribution to what, rather pompously, might be called 'The Concept of *Sergeant*' (and, to a great degree, the others of mine) was very simple:

Sergeant Grimshawe (the ageless William Hartnell) is

about to retire. He has never trained a No. 1 Squad. He's passionately devoted to mould one aided by Corporal Copping (the rock-solid Bill Owen) out of his last intake.

Alas, these National Service conscripts prove to be the Original Awkward Squad - unwilling, uninterested and unlikely to grant him his dream. But, when they hear that Old Leatherlungs has bet his fellow NCOs £50 that he can turn this bunch of dedicated civilians into a unit that even the legendary Guards Regiments would respect, the new soldiers consider:

"Grimshawe shouts. Well, that's what sergeants do. But when has he ever done any of us actual harm? Never."

And so they decide, without fuss, to help him show his fellows he can do it, as well as demonstrate to him that they're not such a gang of incorrigible misfits after all.

This set the style, to a great extent, of the ones I wrote: the incompetent, the uninterested or the plain unlucky, seen at their worst for most of the story, but triumphing in the end, against all expectation, and to rousing effect, in hospital, school, police force, cruise ship and Helping Hands Agency.

So, with *Sergeant* (No. 3 in Britain's box-office returns for 1958, chirpily trailing *Dunkirk* and *The Bridge on the River Kwai* - a well-deserved banner year, cinematically, for the British Army), there we were: with a story thoroughly British in rough-and-ready humour, briefly topped by underplayed sentiment. But ...!

Not until searching my memories for this book, did I realise - thunderbolt! - that ...

The Real Root

... of this film's spirit was a phlegmatically enacted yet breathtaking incident during my Middle East RAF service: a salutary and touching reminder of the fact that every fair-minded serviceman, of whatever rank, knows that it is the Army and RAF sergeants, and their Royal Naval and Royal Marine counterparts, who really, day-to-day, run the armed forces. And, in the process, while all immediate outward appearances are to the contrary, they earn, in due course, and not always retrospectively, an odd but enduring affection.

And now, to wartime Kasfareet, Egypt.

I was a lowly member of the RAF's No. 55 Repair and Salvage Unit (RSU).

All our equipment was sunk along with the SS *Georgic*, in the Red Sea. An emasculated and untried entity, we were taken from Port Tewfik to the massive transit camp at Kasfareet, in Egypt's Canal Zone.

Our young Commanding Officer, a quiet South African engineer, manfully addressed us: without equipment replacement - unlikely to happen quickly - it was a racing certainty that this, his first command, would end before it had begun, and that we would all be summarily disbanded.

But wait! Opposite the Transit Camp there flourished a huge RAF Maintenance Unit (MU), crammed with everything from three-ton trucks to 'Pots, Chamber, Crested, Group Captains For The Use Of'.

A few of 55's sergeants, all long-term regular servicemen, that afternoon strolled across the black, sun-hardened tarmac road to the MU; and gained admission there (impossible without proper written authority) because One Of Ours, in previous years, knew One Of Theirs - the Sgt Guard Commander.

Two similar fortuitous contacts at Sergeant level were chummily exploited at the MU: in the Clerical Section, where all the beloved Forms of Requisition were obtainable; and in Stores Issuing, where such documents were activated.

Within a few hours, our 23-year-old CO was called from his tent, saluted by our Senior Sergeant, and escorted to 55 RSU on spotless parade, in front of a tidy line of lorries, and other new, glistening equipment including a perky little jeep for him.

"Ready when you are, sir," reported our Senior Sergeant.

Thereafter, the unit was covertly known, throughout the RAF Middle East Command as 'Clifty-5 RSU', 'Clifty' being the Arabic for 'thief'.

(Thus, very satisfactorily, two chapters of my life unite in the exercise of sheer, guileless nerve, chutzpah, blarney, call it what you like - RAF and Hollywood, where Mel Brooks deeply impressed me by saying: "On *Your Show of Shows*, the writers' team created a 60-minute comedy script every 7 days. We didn't know it couldn't be done, so we did it.")

Why such effort, at no small risk of grave disciplinary consequences, to hold an untried little unit intact in the midst of a rampant and random war?

It is fashionable to decry the experience of the Blitz, the Battle of Britain, etc. It is also true that these achievements are there, untouched, patiently indifferent to being denigrated by those exercising the freedom that these 'myths' preserve.

A tiny part of the pattern, 55 RSU's NCOs are also there in proof.

A unit of craftsmen, delayed and deprived - but, because of the innate, gruff spirit of the time, not demoralized. I am as sure of this as I am of the fact that the salvage of this salvage unit was an instinctive and unfussy act on the part of those few sergeants, setting a tradition for 55 on which further tradition could be built.

Those I especially recall - 'Chiefy' Price, Warrant Officer Burke and Corporal Flanders (who was recruited in this virtual hijack by the sergeants) - would strenuously deny that it was anything heroic, but merely something unprecedented that had to be done; only they could conceivably do it and so, without fuss, they did it.

As I remember, I didn't give any character in *Sergeant* a nickname. Maybe I should have, inspired by the memory of Flanders who later shot to senior rank in what seemed to be a matter of weeks and was therefore known as 'Poppy The Rocket'.

An Israeli Interlude

An odd echo of *Sergeant* resounded, much later, in Hollywood. Menachem Golan asked me to work on a film about Israeli conscripts and a sergeant he clearly saw as a sort of Moshe Grimsky.

It was difficult for me to accommodate the idea that Israeli conscripts are as resistant to Army discipline as those in far less beleaguered lands. But it is apparently so, and Kosher bullshit is just as noisome as any other.

I admit I couldn't crack this one, nor did I fare better with the next Menachem optimistically offered me:

teenage mayhem at a resort hotel.

I was sorry not to be of help to Menachem whom I first met in London, at director Clive Donner's flat. With partners, Menachem was lugging around Europe, in a battered suitcase, the then bulky reels of his 1965 film, *Sallah*. This told of a Yemeni at odds with Israeli society. It starred an unknown actor with virtually no English, Topol, who took his turn lugging that ton-weight suitcase.

I also cherish Menachem's account of his approach to Ben-Gurion, seeking Government funds to make a major movie.

"Sorry," said the patriarch. "But with that money, we could build ten more villages."

Kenneth Connor

My favourite Sergeant line: the hypochondriac Kenneth Connor character, Horace Strong (nothing subtle in my choice of names), having unknowingly aroused primitive needs in Dora Bryan, is chased by her, past Sgt Grimshawe, who comments:

"Well I'm glad he's useful at something."

Kenneth Connor: in my experience, the least complicated personality in the team. As recruit, part-time cop, injured boxer, ship's doctor, self-appointed secret agent and chemistry teacher, he turned in vigorous, thoughtful and subtle performances in my six. A giant comedy talent, with glimpses of pathos and tenderness, rendered all the more wrenching for their understatement.

How Not to Succeed in Business

Immediately after *Sergeant*, two businesslike consequences were to be expected, both absolutely routine in The Biz, and not calculated to leave hard feelings.

One: Peter would offer me a substantially improved contract.

Two: I would nicely refuse, in order to take up offers from companies now flashing really big money.

One happened - par for the course.

Two? My agent was Peter Eade, as practical and knowledgeable a manager as any in that field, and so gentlemanly that his Cork Street office HQ was once described as possessing the atmosphere of a country solicitor's chambers. In spite of Peter's advice, to move on, and Rita's similar plea (she, with no real experience of The Biz, instinctively knew the score), I metaphorically struck a loyal pose and stayed with Peter Rogers.

Career progressions, in any business, are of obvious, though sometimes overstated importance. An example of the latter, probably apocryphal, but I hope not, is what one Biz pundit said when Elvis Presley died:

"Bad career move."

Okay. So, staying where I was - how was that move rated?

Gerald Thomas said it all, when Peter, unable to believe that I had not responded in the expected manner by rejecting his proposal and heading for other, welcoming doors, asked:

"What's the matter with him, Gerry? Is he mad?"

"No. Just an NJB."

"What's that?"

"Nice Jewish Boy who doesn't want to be thought mercenary."

The Big One - NURSE!

Let me here nail the surprise often expressed, because even an average script, let alone an outstanding one, is written very fast.

No one I know of has ever matched the young Noel Coward penning *Hay Fever* in three days, but this and my drafting of *Carry On Nurse* in ten days should not evoke wonderment any more than did James Joyce spending 17 years on *Finnegans Wake* at the rate of one-and-a-half lines per day. A work takes as long to write as it takes.

So, to recall that *Carry On Nurse* hit the foolscap, virtually unchanged, in a week and a half, is merely to report a statistic, not to make claim for inclusion in any book of records.

Nurses Carrying On

Rita. So many of the film's gags were from her own nursing years, first at Princess Beatrice Hospital, Earls Court, as a student, and then at Hackney General for midwifery (though already an SRN, she was considered a student - at £2 a week), and The Royal Marsden in the operating theatre. And she linked, unforgettably, gratefully, with present members of her profession at the morning Trade Press show.

A public relations master from Anglo-Amalgamated Distributors packed the balcony of Studio One Cinema, in Oxford Street, with a couple of hundred young nurses, just off night duty and half-crazed with fatigue. But not so wiped out that they didn't see every authentic joke coming, begin to laugh and continue laughing through its screening, and for seconds after it was over. What I can only call the 'Ritauthenticity' of so many key scenes received validation from her fellows in gales of innocent merriment that still echo in these old ears.

Not to say that the regular audience didn't respond heartily too. But this first public, deafening reception of *Carry On Nurse* was invaluably endorsed by those exhausted girls. Their presence was an inspired way of validating the film for the rest of the audience. Those young voices, raised to the golden heights of laughter, resonate for me, to this minute.

Acclaim like that happens once in a lifetime or, at any

rate, if ever repeated, never recaptures the elemental force of its first eruption. It is at such rare moments that the most battered movie writer knows that there is a God and that He has a sense of humour.

Paul Dehn, highly civilized critic of the London *News Chronicle*, deemed the notorious daffodil gag to be one of "unsurpassed vulgarity". We met later, at 20th-Century Fox in Beverly Hills, where he was scripting *Planet of the Apes*, and giggled about that remonstrative notice.

Time magazine advised that the picture was ideal entertainment for all who had completed toilet training.

So, a good time was had by all. Especially ...

Hattie Jacques

... whose performance as Matron was, as all the world knows, nothing short of iconic.

She repeated the Matron role in subsequent films and, after her death, I wrote a scene in my too-expensive Again where her framed photograph stood, with all the merited dignity of a battle-honoured dreadnought, on the desk of her successor (*intended to be Joan Sims*) *as a reminder of what a Matron should be.*

Moments in her profoundly effective comedy performances were abrim with the potential of a supremely gifted dramatic actress. Even within a risible situation, when a moment of drama arose, she conveyed all the depth and presence of a sensitive, totally controlled performer. In Hattie there resided, forever uncalled, the capability to give life to Desdemona, Juliet, Lady Macbeth.

Varieties of Bull

Sergeant and *Nurse*, each in its own way, provided me with glancing and proportionate opportunities to tilt at institutionalized and pointless restrictions – also known as bullshit – in both areas of endeavour and service. My view, without diminishing in any way my love and respect for the great services of Nursing and the Armed Forces, is:

When men enlist or are drafted to serve country and cause, I cannot see the need to treat them as recalcitrant halfwits.

Equally, young rigorously trained women, frequently

called upon to take drastic action before a doctor can arrive to tackle a ward emergency, should not be harassed and confined under a series of archaic, hierarchic, meaningless restrictions.

As Hattie commented to me:

"Take this rule about being back in the Nurses' Home by 10 p.m. If a girl is of a mind to lose her virginity some night, Norman, I rather think she'll see to it before 10 o'clock."

Back to School

Viewed again, in America, a few days before writing this, and so many years later, *Carry On Teacher*, overtly the most sentimental of my shows, was still funny, both in its crude slapstick and the measured exchanges between the teachers. Sentimental, of course, because the inciting theme is that the pupils of Maudlin Street School don't want a beloved headmaster to leave, and go to considerable comedic ends to ensure that he doesn't.

Ted Ray, in his sole Carry On appearance, named headmaster William Wakefield his favourite role.

Puzzle: why did the picture do exceptionally well in South America?

My blushiest moment? I wrote "more perfect" for a literate headmaster to say.

Most upsetting? Ten words added to the script - a typical example of hasty on-set action, during production, misfiring in its intention. The pupils' plan, as I've said above, during an official inspection of the school, is to engineer a series of catastrophes so that the headmaster will appear to lack authority and, with this deficiency disapprovingly noted in the official report, the other school will reverse its offer to hire him. When the inspectors arrive, a child's off-screen voice explains:

"These are the ones we have to get rid of."

This is a line I did not write, simply because it completely reverses the children's intention: not to get rid of them but to keep them there long enough to witness a few pupil-made catastrophes and thus decide that the Head had no control over the school. Someone decided that this intention needed to be verbalized - and came up with totally the converse impression.

In short: why not simply telephone the writer and ask

him to supply whatever words are deemed to be necessary?

To be fair, not all writers would co-operate. One, having been paid £20,000 (not a Carry On!) and then thus approached, replied, nicely:

"Sorry, I've been paid for that job and don't owe you any more work on it."

Ted and Joan

Ted Ray: before the film began shooting, he gave me dinner at the Savage Club.

He did not contest a word of the script. All he wanted to say was that he was overjoyed to be given a role that reached beyond Comedy, and to meet with a writer who wasn't afraid to let a page go by without a belly laugh if it enhanced character and, above all, acknowledged the need for the occasional touch of humanizing sentiment.

Joan Sims Carried On plentifully from Nurse onwards, and played the shorts-bursting gym mistress in Teacher. Like Kenneth Williams and myself, she was represented by Peter Eade.

There are those who can't help being funny. To this buoyant

29

band belonged Joan Sims, daughter of the railway stationmaster at Billericay, Essex. (Perennial gag: "She had ideas above her station.")

Within, seriously, she was a sad mass of uncertainties and suffered from more than a touch of the Angosturas - a ferocious bitterness infecting all ranks in The Biz. It arises from the inability to acknowledge that nothing goes on for ever, times and fashions change, and past achievement doesn't earn present support.

"You and I," Joan once intoned to me, in defiant near-tears, "are legends in our own time." I could not resist commenting that, while that might possibly be true, no organisation or individual says to us, every Friday:

"Here's this week's cheque for being a legend."

Joan's love life: so far as one can tell - erratic, trusting and vulnerable. My fancy is that, in contrast to her astute handling of her professional existence during its flourishing years, she yearned to be cherished as a woman and never found this kind of glow.

She died much too young of, I believe, accumulated regret.

But let's close this memory on a livelier and very Joan-esque note, concerning ...

30

Joan and Me

The flattering belief has taken hold in certain dizzy circles that I slept with her. Though scarcely a pivotal controversy in Western history, here are the facts:

Leaving Peter Eade's office in Cork Street - that very London thoroughfare, somehow, almost an extension of the elegance of the Burlington Arcade - we saw an old couple, arm in arm, walking sedately ahead of us, one sunny day.

"Look at that," sighed the sentimental writer, mentally adding Mendelssohn's 'Spring Song' to the soundtrack. "In the twilight of life, still in love, talking over old times. What do you bet they met in this street?"

"What do you bet they're having a row?" said the canny actress.

We passed them as the old lady said:

"Edward, don't talk shit."

Impressed by Joan's instinctive certainty about Life and People, and seeking More Of The Same, I wound up that afternoon at the flat, overlooking Hyde Park that Joan then shared with dancer-choreographer Eleanor 'Fizz' Fazan. We seriously tested the springs of the couch: a shower of kisses, hugs and gropes, but no sexual storm.

Police Work

For *Carry On Constable*, I went to a police station to conduct some mild research, but this depressed me and I didn't start writing until some weeks later.

Then, the formula slipped into gear - a bunch of incompetents, this time reserve cops called in to fill flu-depleted gaps - and worked vigorously enough. The film saw the invaluable, made-to-measure, Carry On-type actor Sid James join the repertory.

And the Ted Ray response was duplicated. Sid asked me to his home: again, I expected some suggestions for radical script changes; again, he was more grateful for what had been written than anxious to achieve changes in it. This time it wasn't so much because of any sentiment accorded the character as relief and pleasure that a rough-spoken Cockney had achieved senior police rank (albeit that Sid was the most gorblimey Cockney ever to emerge from South Africa).

He repeated his gratitude when it came to *Carry On*

Cruising. That a non-posh mariner became Captain of a cruise liner - his role - delighted him even more and indicated to me that, notwithstanding certain relaxation of the emphases in British society, class was still a vital factor at that time - and continues so today.

Diffidence with an Edge

Kenneth Williams excelled in a Constable drag sequence, investigating shoplifting.

I first met him when he was starting out and prone to say earnest things such as:

"The actor's job is to interpret the writer's intention."

That didn't last long.

And nowadays (says Greybeard) new thespians, even in the first flush of innocence, tend not to place any trust in the writer. At the first reading of a stage play of mine, the leading young man once informed me:

"With due respect, I never take any notice of the author's instructions about mood or moves."

One has to admire the odd, glancing use of the word 'respect'.

A born actor and homosexual, Kenny considered his talent essentially uncreative and his orientation so despicable in its physicality that he suffered from a fanatical fastidiousness. He was a glittering wit who took his spiritual and philosophical leanings desperately seriously. And he had the intellectual and literary equipment to do so.

I only once tried conclusions with Ken on the main drive of his life: acting. And got nowhere.

I likened him, in this one area, to Ernest Hemingway. As deeply as I admired Ken's acting (I can never forget him as The Dauphin in St Joan at the Arts Theatre), so did I pay homage to Hemingway's controlled prose. But I had no patience with Mr H's self-lacerating contempt for his writing gift as 'unmanly'. Why did he have to shoot rhinoceroses to compensate for being so effete as to write masterly novels? And refer to any woman under 60 as 'daughter' to reinforce the masculine, generative image? That, I said, was literally balls.

And, equally, there was no reason why Ken couldn't amuse or move thousands, and, if he still felt he was contributing nothing of value to society, do a couple of weeks in a leper colony between engagements - where they'd probably ask him to sing a couple of Rambling Syd Rumpo rural ditties rather than roll bandages.

Customarily professionally fearless, Ken on one occasion

endured agonies over a light romantic scene with Jill Ireland (a subsequent cancer victim). His alternately frustrated and defiant attitude towards sex of the gay kind was as nothing compared to his apprehension over a mild hetero romance scene, no matter how lacking in physical contact (he in a hospital bed; she the visitor, bringing him nougat).

"I'd rather," he told me, "do 'Lear' on stilts."

I reminded him of the trouper who advertised, in The Stage newspaper, "No Known Accent Shirked", but don't claim that this shining example influenced him to settle down and give his all. But he did, acquitting himself nicely, chewing doggedly on the stick-jaw nougat to top the scene.

Kick the Cat

Charles Hawtrey's bizarre claim to special status began when he was impressed by a review, which stated that without him the Carry Ons would not be the same. So he wanted a star on his dressing-room door and top billing in all screening and advertising, etc.

Peter, who always held that the Carry Ons were bigger than any individual involved in them, predictably, disagreed. And, thereafter, Charlie was out.

Hattie Jacques held the opinion that he was eccentric because "what else could you expect from someone who lives with a forgetful mother and an alcoholic cat?"

Did his eccentricity, on and off screen, arise from or depend on alcohol? He was self-admittedly vulnerable, but I never saw him take a drink. In fact when he did a personal appearance at our then local Red Cross at Rickmansworth (Rita was an International Nursing Escort for that organization), he wouldn't even sip sherry at lunch beforehand. And when he'd successfully declared the fête open and they gave him a book by way of modest thanks, this deceptively skilled actor had to turn away to hide the tears.

He gave me the impression, on and off screen, of being two feet off the ground, floating through life. Resolutely eschewing the usual slang implication of the term, one look at Charlie and you had to clap your hands and believe in fairies.

There was certainly a charmed-life confidence about him that nothing could go so wrong that a generous Fate wouldn't correct it, preferably in the nick of time.

To provide background to a pivotal memory of Charlie, I have to break off here and recall …

Myself When Teenaged

... and dreaming - all the time - of being a successful, courted writer, especially when, on teenage West End Saturdays out, passing a building at the corner of Piccadilly and Piccadilly Circus. There, a gleaming brass plate announced that the office of Harry Foster, Theatrical Agent, lay within.

Unfailingly, as I drifted past, I wondered if I would ever enter that office, not beseeching help, but invited because of a spectacular success.

The Carry Ons came - and so did the invitation. And in Mr Foster's office sat producer Ernest Maxin, whose range of talent is fully encompassed by the fact that he has won both the Evening Standard Award for Drama, and the Montreux Award for Comedy.

The eventual result of that meeting was *Our House*, which starred not only Charlie, but Hattie, Joan and Norman Rossington from the Carry Ons.

Peter was pleased for me and, indeed, temporarily released me from our contract to write the ABC Teddington Studios shows.

That's all that's needed to introduce the next Charlie

Hawtrey bit, but I'll take this opportunity just the same to summarize the career of ...

Ernest Maxin

... who is among the most remarkable personalities I have ever met.

In The Biz since he was eight years old, appearing in the Scott and Whaley vaudeville act; former boxer, tipped for a shot at the title in his division; toured Australia with Vivien Leigh in A Streetcar Named Desire, in the course of a considerable acting career; has arranged and conducted recordings of romantic music, as well as presenting a TV show on the same lines, himself as compere and conductor; and post-war producer and director for the BBC and Independent Television - especially fondly remembered for The Morecambe and Wise Show.

I've probably missed out other accomplishments, but won't forget that he has also staged spectacular live summer shows at Blackpool and elsewhere.

My affectionate summary gag is that, for spare-time relaxation, the indefatigable Mr Versatile would play chess with himself, except he can't decide who should win.

Charlie Resumed

Out of many examples of Charlie's tireless application to his craft:

We were stuck for a pay-off line. Ernest and I threw lines and ideas around to no great effect. Charlie finally looked up to say that he had found a line in an early scene that might do it. I won't recount the whole story, but I can assure you that the line - "I've been captured on canvas!" - was the perfect tag. We all enthused. He brushed off all praise.

"It was already there, my dears," he said. "All I did was fall over it."

(All performers of instinct and quality know this innocent feeling. Ray Charles once tolerantly said to Jamie Foxx: "How can you misplay that chord? It's right there, under your fingers.")

How do I most vividly remember him? Far away from scripts, rehearsal rooms or studios.

At the wedding of Ernest and actress/dancer Leigh Madison, I caught swift sight of Charlie as the couple walked down the aisle on their way out. He leant forward, propping both arms on the pew in front, intent on them, unblinking, and his head a little to one side, like a warm, inquisitive puppy. He wore a grossly unsuitable Anthony Eden hat and a long dark overcoat that he considered suitable for a synagogue ceremony.

And, in his eyes, there was a luminous tenderness that I had never seen in him before. It wasn't envy; it was childlike wonder. It wasn't sadness; it was joy for these two in love and for all who have ever loved or will love. Then he caught me looking at him and dropped the expression as if it were scorching his face with the undouseable flame of truth.

Courage of a high order attended his passing. He suffered from that vicious ambush of a disease - diabetes. As I heard it, his only chance of survival was amputation of both legs. He preferred death.

The Indispensable Element ...

... in life is Luck.

Napoleon demonstrated his respect for this dictum when the qualities of a young officer were recited to him, with a view to winning the man promotion. He was brave, resourceful, a natural leader, loyal, secure in tactics and military history, etc. Bonaparte listened to it all, then asked:

"Ah - but is he lucky?"

Likewise, The Biz.

So I can say, plain fact, that I was vastly lucky to be in at the beginning of 'The Phenomenon', the Carry Ons, because the first four of my half-dozen scripts were aimed, with relish, at towering British institutions, with the audience needing no reminder of their ready-made comic aspects.

The very word 'sergeant' instantly evokes, in Britain, the image of a profane, shouting and eventually madly memorable and likeable tyrant, his blood circulation impeded by ingrowing stripes.

Say 'bedpan' and the hallowed image of UK hospitals - glowing nurses, glowering matrons, libidinous men - fades in, clear and sharp.

And one cannot mention the police force or school without similar eternal British atmospheres and stereotypes jostling for jovial inclusion.

Public familiarity with the subject, then, was everything, or at least urgently desirable. Well-meaning people, moved by their own enthusiasms, could not grasp, when suggesting we do (say) *Carry On Stock Exchange*, that we'd have to spend time at the beginning of such a film explaining the unfamiliar market before we could make fun of it.

And *Carry On Angling* promised to be rather static: "Someone falls in the water - then what?"

So, *Sergeant* set the pioneering course, including fade-out sentiment à l'anglais, with upper lip flash-frozen.

The Last But One

With *Regardless* came change, principally and crucially, for me, in the format. Where once we played recognizable havoc with sergeants et al., now we had a Helping Hands Agency which, while not outlandish, was not an institution habitually used by the general public. While (laboriously to make the point once again) every cinema-goer had been to school, probably in the Services, or in a hospital, not so many, one could safely assume, had ever hired someone to take a pet monkey for a walk.

Regardless, therefore, was, by its very nature, suited to episodic, unconnected comedy sketches rather than an ongoing story.

This is not to say that the chimp sequence wasn't

funny (Ken Williams, as the simian's escort, carried it off with unruffled social charm), but it was outside general experience. Funny? - yes. Familiar, à la previous Carry Ons? - no.

There was a thread: the gang feared eviction from the agency's premises and was repeatedly visited by a gobbledegook-speaking landlord (Stanley Unwin).

And there was one sequence with which I was very happy, and has kindly been called classic: Kenneth Connor misunderstanding an assignment (where would comedy be without misunderstanding?) to the extent of believing, thrilled, that it involved him in the Secret Service. Moreover, it put him on a train destined to cross the Forth Bridge, a clear link with the mysterious shenanigans of *The 39 Steps*.

Regret: the censor would not permit a sequence, lavish with double meanings, that put Charles Hawtrey into a woman's wardrobe to overhear and report on her talking in her sleep.

It's pointless, I suppose, to protest that generations of hearty stage farces, at the Aldwych Theatre and elsewhere, with far more suggestive situations didn't undermine public morality.

Sailing into the Sunset

Cruising did have plot coherence and comedy chances of the *Sergeant/Nurse* kind. However, cruising wasn't then as widespread a British holiday style as it has since become. But, I'm bound, happily, to record that this didn't diminish its box-office appeal.

It was the first Carry On in colour and my last in any tint. And, after this, the trend of the series was more towards unbridled fantasy (*Cleo*) and earthiness (*Convenience*). Twenty of these big hits were written by the tirelessly inventive Talbot Rothwell.

In comedy, all is unpredictable. The biggest and most unexpected laugh in *Cruising* always came with this:

Ship's Officer: "What's afoot?"

Ship's Doctor: "It's that funny-shaped thing at the end of your leg."

Why?! Don't ask me. Refer instead, please, to Robert McCrum, author of the quite marvellous biography of P.G. Wodehouse, who simply says:

"All comedy rebuffs serious analysis."

With that, let the good ship *Carry On Cruising* and my memories of it, and the five 'Vessels of Laugh' that preceded it, sail, a fleet of fun, serenely into the sunset, truly, finally unsinkable.

Tradition

A Hollywood producer, reacting to accusations that he had been unwise to buy the rights of some book or other, indignantly hit back:

"It has stood the test of time for six whole months."

Always modest, what P-G and I accomplished can confidently be said to have entered into, and stayed in, British tradition for rather longer, even if, largely, this has happened because we were inspired by the tradition itself. Ready British identification with the early Carry On themes, in my lucky six, was hearteningly demonstrated many times. I'll mention only three:

* A nurses' strike was averted. The *Daily Express* headlined, front page: 'CARRY ON NURSE'.

* Laurence Olivier, in Shaw's *The Devil's Disciple*, got the film's least expected laugh when he had to order

"Carry on, Sergeant!"

* Dilys Powell, *Sunday Times* super-critic, speaking on BBC radio's *The Critics* about some serious medical drama, bluntly declared that she preferred *Nurse* because it was honest and robust.

What Might Have Been

When the turn began to happen, I dutifully did a script of *Carry On Spying*. And I must confess that, in my dour view (never mind P-G's for the moment), it was so unsatisfactory that I never want it to see the merciless light of day. That some - a very few - liked it, is only comforting to a degree and made no difference anyway. On this showing, P-G and I parted.

For some time after, admittedly still a little broody but tiring of the brackish taste of licked wounds, I persuaded myself that I simply was not equipped to work on the new Carry Ons anyway - temperamentally, stylistically, call the lack what you will - and that was that. But, as time did its stuff in England as in Casablanca, and went by at the usual rate, I reached a less abashed conclusion and self-confidence was rousingly restored.

Peter, after all, at those first story conferences, used to say, "You can write anything." So, with perhaps something more than competence and a lot less than genius (though Peter has twice, recklessly, called me such), I have, over the busy and satisfying years, penned a Shakespearean blank-verse historical play, and another stage piece so controversial, apparently, that it has not yet found a home in London, medical dramas, crime/detection, camp adventure, magic realism et al., picking up an award or two on the way. And there was, strangely, a consequence I have never before revealed. (See "Carry Ons" While You Wait, below).

For the Record

Not my idea and, in my memory it doesn't even have a title, but the London office of an American company, either prompted by P-G or off its own baseball bat, became interested in the notion of combining the styles of two established comedy series - the Carry Ons and the Hope-Crosby Road pictures.

This time, The Road would lead to the Moscow of perestroika and glasnost, travelled by appropriate comedians facing appropriate obstacles.

I was in London at the time and, with Gerry, met the American lady exec once or twice. All I can honestly summon from memory is that she wanted a pie-throwing sequence. This is not to say that she was bereft of other story ideas, but that's the only particular I can summon from this brief episode.

Also vanished from sight is the Story Outline I wrote at that time, wherein custard pies were duly hurled with abandon, along with any hope of that courageous 'Carry On Along the Road to Moscow' (or whatever it was to be called) ever taking even a faltering step towards production.

Columbus

Hold on. I didn't write this one. But hearken, just the same. There's a tale to be told.

All I actually know of its production circumstances is what its veteran writer Dave Freeman told me at the 40th Carry On anniversary lunch: he was under constant pressure to turn in pages because of the overriding aim of reaching the target release date of 4 July in the USA.

It doesn't take a literature don to deduce that the best writing, or judgement of it, is not customarily achieved under such obsessive goading. However, there is a classic case - *Casablanca* - which 'turned out all right' even though no one at Warners knew what they would be filming until the pages arrived daily on the set, having been written overnight and probably out of sequence.

(I'm also given to understand that Jack Warner wanted to cut something from the film: the song 'As Time Goes By'. I'm not jeering at that error. As Peter Rogers said, quoted at the beginning of these reminiscences: "We all make mistakes." And, as William Goulding trenchantly observed, about film-making in general: "Nobody knows anything.")

Anyway, the miracle of *Casablanca* buoys up film-makers to this day when caught, for whatever reason, in a chase-your-tail production situation. And expediency outweighs logic. But miracles, by definition, can't be ordered on the call sheet, and *Columbus* anyway, I think it might be agreed, even potentially, was no *Casablanca*.

Without commenting on the *Columbus* plot and the inhibiting factor that the cast, though gifted, just wasn't the vintage line-up, I sorrowfully felt, from the beginning and afar, that Americans would not look tolerantly on any foreigners' comedic treatment of their country's hallowed discoverer.

This conviction was reinforced by the then recent experience of Steve Walsh (see Pine and Holly) and myself that Spain did not welcome filming on its territory of any version, however respectful, of *Don Quixote*, other than the original text, by Spain's Shakespeare, Miguel Cervantes. And if they prefer me to refer to Shakespeare as Britain's Cervantes, in any unlikely Hispanic edition of this slim volume - respectfully, and ever amenable, I agree.

I don't know how *Columbus* did in the USA and if it was a respectable box-office take, but I couldn't be more pleased if I tried.

The first I knew of the project was a colour spread in the *L.A. Times* magazine.

I didn't take it too well, even though by then (as above) I'd bounced back from the severing of my relationship with the Carry Ons.

I just thought it might have crossed someone's mind, when looking for a writer for this Carry On, that the fellow who wrote the first six and, moreover, had by then lived in the USA for a good number of years, might have been considered fairly suitable for the job. I mean, like, some degree of horses for courses, might have been indicated?

Fortunately, by then, I had at least learned not to splutter phoned-in indignation into unreceptive and embarrassed ears. So I left it until I next saw Gerry Thomas, in England. He assured me that they had thought "at once" of me, but the stumbling block was my membership of the Writers' Guild of America etc., etc., and in four words, it was no go.

At dinner, I told him that, for fun, as soon as I'd heard of the film, I'd scribbled an opening scene for *Columbus*, which, in my view, would have set it in the comfortably and recognizably traditional groove as in *Sergeant* and *Cruising*: the viewer would meet the cast as, lined up on the deck of the *Santa Maria*, Columbus interviewed them as to their suitability to be his crew on the voyage.

There and then, with an evident and touching anticipation, Gerry read the following:

Columbus: "Why do you want to discover a New World?"

1st Applicant: "I want to take one of Sicily's most cherished institutions out there and found an organization which will supply whatever the people want - happy snorting-powder, vino, signorinas - but forbidden by Puritan laws. I will protect that organization with ruthless dedication and a solid hidden base of corrupted carabinieri."

Columbus: "Bene, bene! What's your name?"

1st Applicant: "Capone."

Columbus: "And you?"

2nd Applicant: "Signor - I have a dream - to lead the Government, and protect it, and especially myself, with all means and plumbers at my disposal. A flood of benefits will accrue to the people, unstoppable by any gate - especially a water one."

Columbus: "Name?"

2nd Applicant: "Nixon."

Columbus: "You're in. Report to the galley. Clearly, you're good at cooking things up. Next?"

3rd Applicant: "I want to sell gloves, then move into making dramas for the people, mangle the language and ..."

Columbus: "Good enough. Name?"

3rd Applicant: "Goldfisch."

Columbus: "Change it."

3rd Applicant: "Goldwyn?"

Columbus: "Magnifico! Americans wouldn't buy anyone called Gold-lose. You, compadre?"

4th Applicant: "Actually, old boy, I'm English, not Spanish, haw-haw doncherknow? Son of the sea, hearts of oak and all that rot. Superbly placed to supply trouble-free, non-union labour to the burgeoning industries of the New World. You - er - cotton on?"

Columbus: "I think so. But what do you call your system?"

4th Applicant: "Slavery."

Columbus: "A fine European tradition for all you're an Inglese faggio. Welcome. You?"

5th Applicant: "I believe in private enterprise and want to compete with Gold-whoever. The name's Warner."

Columbus: "You don't look like you could handle it alone."

5th Applicant: "I have two brothers."

Columbus: "Bring 'em along. It's a big country."

5th Applicant: "How do you know, capitano?"

Columbus: "I've seen the movie. Bene."

6th Applicant: "How did you know my name?"

Columbus: "Who the Dante's Inferno are you? Bene who?"

6th Applicant: "Goodman."

Columbus: "Swingin'! Bring your flute. Pipe me aboard. That's it for today. Carry On."

All Applicants: "Si, si!"

Columbus (in close-up, choked with emotion): "Already they love me enough to refer to me by my initials ...?"

Voracious and sharp-eyed perusers of the *Carry On* library will remember that the above scene has previously been published in a Richard Webber book.

Cringing with modesty, I hope it's worth reading twice and, anyway, in this book leads rather nicely to:

Carry Ons While You Wait

Or rather, while *I* waited.

For what?

The fondly dreamt-of call to come on home, one day, from Holly to Pine, and take a crack at writing one of the "new" Carry Ons, especially those which, merrily and disrespectfully, took on historical themes and personalities, as in "Cleo" and "Don't Lose Your Head." And I'd be ready because, **and I reveal this now, here, for the first time ...**

... as soon as self-deprecation wore off, I periodically, over the years, thought up and noted suitable premises. And kept them to myself, against the day ...

... which, predictably, to anyone but a cloudy melodramatist like myself, was clearly not even on the most distant horizon. There *was* a call, back to the dear old studio - to repeat myself, with "Carry On Again, Nurse" (the 'too-expensive' version), but not to test the judgement that the new style was not within my range.

As you read on, about my rather odd and powerful family background, you may judge whether this secret stockpiling of Carry On notions was evidence of the lingering effects of Hudism - Hudis Hubris In Extremis - or ... ?

Not that it matters now. It's probably as simple as the verdict that follows: you can take the writer out of the Carry Ons but not the Carry Ons out of the writer.

Thus, crazily perhaps, I let my fancy roam free – as to How I Could Have Carried On, If Asked – on various original themes. All ready for The Call which, predictably, never came.

Columbus was the first of these jolly exercises.

After the standard cast-intro parade, we'd set sail – and discover that (say) six of the very motley crew have smuggled their girls aboard. This worked nicely for Pte. Monkhouse in "Sergeant" on dry land, with one girl involved: why not six times as well on the bounding main?

Anyway, it takes little raunchy imagination to envision what the poster-artists would wrought with the images of six busty girls and their lusty Latin males swarming all over the celebrated vessel, popping out of portholes and, implicitly, shagging in the lifeboats.

But, in my scheme, the ladies had, as a unit, a more final and feminist role to play. Like this:

Superstition and fear become rife among the men, to the point of mutiny. Object: turn back before we either a) get swallowed by dragons rearing out of the unknown waters or b) simply sail off the edge of the flat earth.

However, both C.C. and the crew reckon without Les Girls. Ever more practical than their frothing menfolk, and hearing of the impending rebellion, they move in and take over. Forget the mutiny! They haven't come this far to abandon the hope of material riches awaiting all in the New World.

Pausing only to fight off The Pirates Of Penzance (who sing, not speak, all their dialogue, Gilbert and Sullivan style, including a tongue-twisting breakneck Carry On version of "A Modern Major-General"), it's yo-ho-ho and a cask of sherry and in an exhilarating burst of gale-driven speed, they land in New York.

There they are met by a dusty-smocked beret-sporting character, wielding hammer and chisel, who greets them with:

"Salud! Where do you want ze Statue Of Liberty?"

Maybe you can resist. But I can't. The memory of it all is both hilarious and poignant. So let's give a first-time-ever peek into two more phantom Carry Ons, intended as Couldabeens, but finished up as Neverwases.

Created, surely, for a vintage Carry On, is the British Seaside. My Carry On treatment would have celebrated two formidable institutions: the Concert Party and the Boarding House.

This company of doughty entertainers, far from Good Companions, duplicate all the petty and passionate temperaments, envies and schemings of back stage.

They lodge at stage-struck Hattie Jacques' boarding house where Kenneth Williams harbours a hopeless passion for the majestic landlady. I planned to give Kenny his movie-part of a lifetime: as a mime, who never speaks because he's forever, in and out of performance, perfecting his art: the English version of Jean-Louis Barrault's tormented Baptiste in "Les

Enfants du Paradis."

And Good Parts For All: Leslie Phillips the company Lothario with undying dreams of yet becoming a West End matinee idol – Ken Connor as a virtually suicidally depressed but uproarious comedian – and wardrobe mistress Joan Sims as the all-purpose understudy, ready at the drop of a temperature to step even into male shoes.

Backstage, did I say? Not so. Because this never-say-die-troupe has no stage to get in back of. They appear on the very sands. This would give the movie its title:

"Carry On Under The Pier if Wet."

It's been asserted that John Huston made "Moulin Rouge" not out of any overriding interest in Toulouse-Lautrec, but because he wanted to film the Can-Can.

So I'm in excellent cinematic company when I declare that I'm quite happy to be accused of fantasizing about "Carry On Shylock Holmes" solely to be able to pen its projected final line of dialogue.

To this end, I would have turned the Doyle images on their heads: Shylock H would be blithely thick-headed, while Dr Wattstein, sworn from birth to shield his daft cousin from the consequences of his opium-wreathed incompetence, actually possesses all the boundless esoteric knowledge and the inspired flair for detection.

Why the Jewish aspect? Certainly, I would not have overplayed this, and used it only for generally comprehended laughs. And all would have worked toward the moment at the very end, when, in utter pent-up exasperation the hitherto incredibly patient medic rounds on S.H. with:

"Elementary – *you schmuck.*"

Honest Envy

Hearing that Rita and I were in London, Terry Johnson invited us to his 1998 National Theatre hit play about the Carry Ons.

In a last-minute rush, we unerringly hailed the one taxi driver in London who couldn't find the right entrance to the theatre.

So we were ten minutes late for the show, which doesn't need me to validate it as deft in observation, free in imagination and lavish in comedy ideas and, especially, razor-edged dialogue. We met the electrifying cast - heart-shaking reincarnations of Williams, James and Windsor, who looked on us with touching deference.

I called Terry Johnson the next morning - in the midst of his conferring with the police about death threats he had received. That development, he agreed, was quite unexpected. For myself, I wish those so lethally offended by the play had taken their lead from Barbara Windsor: frankly characterized on that stage, she commented openly, after seeing the show, that she wasn't in the least dismayed.

To preface the following note, I quote a review by Katherine Chetkovich, in *The Observer* of 22 July 2003: "This is a story about two writers, in other words of envy."

I frankly and honestly envy two writers, for fastening on to two rich subjects: Peter Shaffer, for *Amadeus*, the germ of which was around for decades in a seven-page playlet by Pushkin; and Terry Johnson for his masterly development of a subject that, to quote Ray Charles again, "was right there under my fingers" from the moment of its inception. I'm not saying I could have written as stunningly as them, but, as Sean Penn says, about The Biz in general:

"You may fail - but you gotta try."

Having strayed on to the live stage, it's fitting that we stay there for a little while because ...

An Enjoyable but Expensive Mistake

... is very much part of the extremely fertile Early Carry On period. (I'm beginning to think of the whole thing as a sort of cinematic geological Age.)

The episode can be summed up in a four-letter word: 'Andy'.

But it began with a Berwydd and continued with a Gwyn.

When we lived in Rickmansworth, Herts, I was interviewed by a veteran journalist, Berwydd Davies of the *Watford Observer*. He asked if he could introduce a fellow-Welshman to me: Gwyn Arch, grammar school English and Music teacher, and a restless composer.

We clicked as a team from the start.

Result: a stage musical, *Andy*.

And I've rarely had as much fun and excitement as I

revelled in during this collaboration.

Andy was a simple and (fatally - read on!) original tale of (now one must add) pre-AIDS philandering. The anti-hero, compulsive womanizer Andy Mills, is an assistant director in TV and films, with a desert-dry approach to his work:

"Yeh - this series is a breakthrough - from drivel to muck."

He shares a flat with Wilfred Nelson, schoolteacher.

Right. Gwyn and I wrote of what we knew. So far all's well.

Script, lyrics and music completed, in a breezy flurry, we recruited a group of young singers for the demo tape and a few live performances for prospective backers, for which we rented the Fortune Theatre. My sister Sylvia, with ambitions as a singer at the time, participated in the chorus work and, especially effectively, soloing a very sad song, 'Blue Dawn'.

At one of these showings - bare stage, no props, reading from scripts, small group of musicians - the representative of a certain mogul expressed himself "moved", especially by the driving rhythm and harsh words of the showpiece, 'Never Mention Love', but counselled:

"If you can use these great melodies, with new lyrics, for another show, based on a best-seller or a well-known real-life story, then you might stand a chance, for all you're a new team. But this is a tough business."

Gotcha. So that was 'The Mistake'. Exhilarated by the flow of our seamless, inventive collaboration, we failed to realize:

That most musicals (partly to encourage backers that the show in question is not a total gamble and, to some extent, is pre-sold to the public) stem from established sources.

Witness, successfully (*My Fair Lady* from *Pygmalion*) and otherwise (*Twang!* from Robin Hood). And even *West Side Story* went through too many depressing auditions before hitting its classic stride. I have to mention, a little wearily perhaps, that the obvious candidate, *Casablanca*, though worked on by Lerner and Loewe (*Camelot*) with the film's writers, never made it to the stage.

All of the above - is it merely our huffy excuse for the

rejection of a lousy script/score/story? I don't think so. Our work would have doubtless benefited from revision during rehearsal and tour, as always. But too many people, of some authority, praised it. It seems fair to conclude: the fact that the story was original - a plus in almost any other field - went a long way to damn it as a commercial musical proposition.

We got one bite. A brave young American, David Kitchin, took a modest option. His plan was first to present a stage play and then, with the presumed profit, back *Andy*. Prudent, but still a gamble. Which he didn't win.

The play closed before it could reach London.

We obviously never got to do a tour, but nevertheless sympathize with celebrated writer and play-doctor George Kaufman: on tour, stuck for an idea, he entered a haberdashery store and enquired:

"Do you have any second act curtains?"

We've stayed in touch with Jane and Gwyn Arch, he now 'retired' to a busy life in music, composing and conducting.

Never Young

Andy still sings powerfully and demandingly, via the riveting taped voice of David Watson.

At audition, this slender youth (a classically trained and gifted pianist) sight-read the score and SANG - boom! - with astounding, commanding resonance, dominating, on a bare stage.

We became friends. He was in Hollywood, trying his luck, when we arrived. We rejoiced with him when he sang *Candide* in Los Angeles and starred as Strauss Jr, in *The Great Waltz* at Drury Lane (not far from the Fortune Theatre ...)

David is now a top agent in London - top because he's been through it all and knows all the jokes and the pitfalls, from deep personal experience: the vivid extremes of standing, auditioning, alone and unknown on an empty stage - and, alone again, but accepting a standing ovation and a typically impulsive hug from Leonard Bernstein.

Abiding memory: we were driving along 26th Street, Santa Monica, one evening. We saw an entwined and entranced couple strolling.

A stab of regret, reliving my smug Hudisian chastity.

"I was never that young, David."

David Watson said: "I still am."

The Prolific One

Talbot Rothwell, Carry On writer after I left, was a police officer turned pilot turned writer - the last when he was a prisoner of war in Germany.

His line, in *Cleo* -

"Infamy! Infamy! They've all got it in for me!"

- could not be more English if it were printed in red, white and blue and served with a complimentary Yorkshire pudding.

It's been voted the funniest line ever in a British comedy. This was reported, among many other places, in a British expatriate newspaper in Los Angeles and I sent the clipping to Peter, for Tolly's family, to assure them that, wherever Britons were scattered, he and the Carry Ons were not forgotten.

I only met him once - for barely a minute. I tremble to claim parity, but, to a small extent, the encounter matched the immortal moment when Wilde and

Beerbohm crossed each other's paths on a morning walk in Covent Garden. Onlookers held their breaths for an unforgettable exchange of wit. This is what they heard:

"Hello, Oscar."

"Hello, Max."

In our case, by utter accident, and cornily fitting, I was leaving the Carry On office as he was approaching it.

"Hi. I'm Norman Hudis. You must be ...?"

"Talbot Rothwell."

"Good luck."

"You too."

I can't vouch for it fully, but have been told that, towards the end, he was too ill to attend at the studios and all script conferences took place at his home.

He retired from writing because of ill-health and died on 28 February 1981.

The Price

Earlier, I told of Gerry's wistful reading of my *Columbus* opening scene. He asked, quietly:

"Why didn't you send it to us?"

"Because," I said, equally gently, "you once chided me for being too eager to please."

(A sensitivity which, as related above, compelled me to make notes for possible Carry Ons but, God forbid, never offer them to P-G after the break.)

Then, on an impulse from nowhere, I asked him the major question.

"Gerry. Tell me. During all that time on the Carry Ons, were you ever at ease?"

"Never. Not for five minutes."

Gerald Thomas died on 9 November 1993. Massive attack. Heart.

BEGINNINGS: FAMILY

THE HINDSIGHT SAGA

The Key

If I'd paid more attention in my few Hebrew classes, I'd have likely deduced that since my father's name, Isaac, means 'laughter', my family might, earlier, have been perceived by me not so much as a dangerously misleading influence, but more a slightly alarming, self-perpetuating JOKE.

This part-helpful conclusion took years to arrive. I'll tell of the circumstances, with pleasure, later.

For now, I won't say that this refreshing slant alone fashioned me as a comedy writer. However, it most certainly reinforced my recognition of 'The Absurd'.

Nevertheless, is there a serious 'psychological' root to Hudism?

Of course. Quite simple too.

Massive insecurity leading to the concerted, unending attempt to counter it.

The Hudises, or Hudi as I'll occasionally call them, to impart a slight classical note to the proceedings, were British-born of European Jewish immigrants. Their parents brought insecurity with them in their luggage. The children, my father and siblings, inherited it.

73

But also, crucially, denied it, and erected a towering wall of fantasy, achievement, morality, omniscience and exclusivity to shut it out.

And patrolled that wall 24/7.

QED (= Quite Enough Damage.) Stay tuned.

Maturity While You Wait - Half a Lifetime

The Vicomtesse Marie-Laure de Noailles had the jolting habit of asking new acquaintances:

"At what age did you become yourself?"

Me, madame? Not yet, entirely. My process takes place in periodic hopeful stumbles towards understanding. One has had to find the urge, from time to time, sanely to evaluate the family's giant Aesop fables, complete with expositions and morals. Not the least of these is ...

Isaac's Sacrifice, or The Incomplete Gesture

Dad's three brothers became The Teacher, The Civil Servant and The Estate Agent, and routinely sneered at him as The Tailor because he had to go into their father's workshop. (This scorn did not inhibit them, lifelong, from obtaining bespoke suits and overcoats from him for the price of the cloth, if that.)

Knuckling under because "If I argued with my father, my mother would break down", Jack decided that if this was his lot, he'd at least be the best tailor he could. He studied, therefore, at the Sir John Cass Technical Institute, in the East End, and developed into a first-class cutter and, eventually, production manager (Government award for rationalizing the production of battledress in the Second World War).

And he hated his work, throughout his life, since he should plainly have been an engineer of fame, or at least a happy auto mechanic.

Fiery disputes, predictably, erupted with his impossible autocratic father.

During one, Jack rushed from the house and returned with a steerage ticket for New York, leaving in a few hours. That's it. Goodbye.

As confidently forecast, under this stress, his mother went to pieces. There's no telling what he would have done had she blessed his departure - a very intriguing speculation. But she obliged with sobs and, under that stress, Isaac known as Jack flung the ticket into the fire.

The ritual Hudisian drama was complete:

* Act 1 - provocation and conflict.

* Act 2 - defiance, teetering confidently on the edge of flamboyant exit.

* Act 3 - self-sacrifice, nobly to stem a mother's tears.

There were, as my astute and late brother Michael (an inspired History teacher, and beloved of wife Pat), eventually pointed out, no witnesses to this Yiddish Theatre scene. But there don't need to be. It contains the necessary ingredients for Hudisian fulfilment: magnificent gesture, recognized but unmentioned by all concerned, as signifying nothing.

Rather more documented, there's the ...

Incident in Glasgow

... where Jack got his best job ever and which, at its doleful nadir, damn near killed him.

So simpatico was he with the boss that a partnership was early mooted.

But a true Hudis can't merely count a blessing. The Fundamentals of the Faith decree that he must share it, and be seen doing so.

And so, from London, two families within the Hudis orbit (but not echt Hudi) were urgently invited to Glasgow, the dads taking good jobs at the factory in question.

I never got the full story but, from hints a mile wide, one of the London beneficiaries appeared to have screwed up, probably innocently but definitely irreversibly. Everybody had to go back to London.

In our case, penniless.

Perforce, we stayed with an Aunt Supreme, who, in this ghastly extreme, applied family ties quietly and nobly, accepting and sharing the burden - crucially, unHudis - without judgement.

Jack, economizing even on bus fares, left her demure, now-overcrowded suburban semi-detached daily before dawn: walked, job hunting, all over London; barely ate; reeled through a near-fatal bout of flu; and finally found a job and a flat. And none of this in any way was staged, floodlit heroism, to be renounced as soon as announced (as in 'The Case of the Burning Steerage Ticket'), but the real bloody thing.

Though, operating fully-fledged-and-pledged Hudism, all this was strictly his own nepotistic fault, it would be a mercilessly sullen son-nephew who failed to acknowledge that Dad and his sister rose to this occasion flawlessly.

So I'm happy to write, with huge relief, the humble tribute that:

Jack was a good Dad, fallen among Hudises.

But he'd have been better off, when young and unattached, in New York, 3,000 miles from the whole stultifying pack and the unyielding stress of Hudism.

When I took Rita and young Stephen and Kevin to America, Jack hugged me and choked out:

"What pluck!"

As if I were plunging into the unknown as an unknown - as he, in fantasy at least saw himself when young - when in fact I went by invitation and took some reputation with me.

The exact moments when, savingly, the-Hudi-as-a-JOKE hit me with the certainty of collision, are clear and revered.

A Start

At the Bel Air Hotel, Los Angeles, I was interviewed as a prospective writer by a team of Procter and Gamble executives responsible for that company's soap-opera productions. It went nicely. They finally asked me 'the diligence question': was I comfortable, as a writer, with the style and substance of these daytime series, or did I, secretly, scorn them?

My reply developed into a virtual stand-up comedy monologue - deadpan delineation of Hudism, with pungent character examples and incidents.

The conclusion: the eccentricities of my family equalled and sometimes outstripped almost any emotional plot-turn that soap opera could come up with. Not a word was untrue or exaggerated.

Nor was it tragic.

Bill Cosby rather than Ibsen.

I left them laughing - and drove away on Stone Canyon Road, strangely uplifted. Epiphany? Rather, I think, it was the epicentre of a moral and emotional earthquake.

Till then, for all my years, I'd gone along, solemnly,

dutifully, with the demanding creed of Hudism, and never once cast an amused eye at it. Now I had, and knew I could, and so I began to exorcise it.

But just the same I realized:

You don't reverse, in a day or a week, the inexplicable surrender, for years, to family demands so extreme and absurd that most people would have fled home at age 12 - at the latest. But, as the old gag goes, like 24 lawyers at the bottom of the sea, this was a start.

Shamefully late. Why?

I've given much space to assessing people important in my life. But, at this point, I feel bound to devote a few cautious lines to ...

My View of Me

I was so precociously obsessed with getting out of school and into work, in some capacity as a writer, that, while not entirely unaware of the oddity of my upbringing, I felt I could postpone dealing with its subtle influence until the first priority had been achieved. This, I'm content to agree, is the AAF theory - Arse About Face - of human development. And my crisp self-diagnosis of me is, simply:

"Not so much mea culpa as mea twitta."

I trust we have reached a point where, armoured, to some extent, against the heavy, we can invoke a lighter touch and take on board ...

The Six Commandments of Hudism

... which, need I say, are more wordy than the original Ten.

* ONE: thou shalt NEVER cause thy father and thy mother a moment's unease, and moreover thou shalt therefore strive to bring home the equivalence, or the actuality thereto, of at least one scholarship a week.

* TWO: thou shalt acknowledge that all Hudi behaviour and opinions are superior and immutable.

* THREE: thou shalt in thy work behave, at all times, in the confident offhand spirit of "It's on your desk, sir" and - lo! - thus induce shock and awe in thine employer and gnashing of teeth among patently inferior employees.

* FOUR: if a boy, thou shalt ever be aware of what cometh to pass if thou lyeth carnally with maidens: yea,

disease; or, double-yea, rendering her with child; or - oh thrice yea! - even both; and perchance there may come to pass an enforced and tainted marriage of unparalleled woe in a distant town where, alack, of Hudi there are none. If thou art a girl child, all of the above applieth, only more so and with especially prolonged and painful labour.

(This one is reduced in the Concise Version to: "Thou shalt beg God to see to it that no young Hudi learns about life by living it.")

* FIVE: know thou then, boy, that when the right maiden, so to speak, uh, cometh, she will be instantly recognized as such by thee, even as a flash of lightning illumines a dark sky. Verily shall she be temperate, thrifty, virginal, even unto pursed lip and vinegary aspect. Hear ye, further, that Divorce, an admission of failure due to imperfection, cannot, by definition, happen to a Hudi.

* SIX: ever shalt thou be proud that the Hudi, ahead in all things, need only six Commandments.

I'll be surprised if elements of all this are not recognized by many people from their own histories.

Some may even identify all symptoms and practices of Hudism within their own family experience. I hope so, because, surely, no one family can possibly monopolize the entire dizzy spectrum. I'm almost certain, however, that most people's escape routes have been earlier accomplished and far less complex than mine.

Who Is Sylvia?

At this familial point – due and loving tribute to my sister.

Sylvia Anne Hudis rebelled, impressively and honourably, much earlier than I did, against strangulating Hudism or, to be extremely accurate, Pollyjackism arising from Hudism as a sort of slightly breakaway sect. Her most drastic repudiation of and action against the complacent future charted by them for her, went spectacularly wrong from the start and redirected her life into deprivation and betrayal: a grim and relentless proof that hell is the destination when the road is paved with impeccable intentions.

This was post-war. During WWII, Sylvia distinguished herself in the WAAF. As a Wireless-Telephone

Operator, guiding often battered malfunctioning bombers home, she was on duty, alone, at one of the small outposts devoted to this duty. One returning aircraft was so disabled that it could have crashed anywhere on its home base, as likely as not on Sylvia's lonely little building. Aircraftwoman Hudis S.A., promptly got under the small ops table, for its scant protection and continued broadcasting to the stricken aircraft. She was briskly commended by the Commanding Officer.

The incident is, almost cornily, typical of Sylvia throughout her later years of ceaseless struggle. No matter how hazardous and terrifying her situation, she took whatever shelter was available – or scorned the often complete lack of it – and continued performing what she considered to be her plain duty.

She is rewarded by the blessing of having gifted, supportive and loving children.

Which leaves the question: who am I to make these claims and judgements, even conceding that they are inevitably subjective and imperfect?

A legitimate query. And in response I can only

modestly say that I am a better judge of my topic than two noteworthy pundits in other fields, namely:

* The record company execs who rejected The Beatles because: "We don't like their sound and, anyway, guitar groups are on the way out."

* And the First World War German Army Personnel Officer who concluded an evaluation with:

"He lacks qualities of leadership."

He was referring to Cpl Adolf Hitler.

Mama in the Cathedral

I dare not even attempt to talk for the other offspring, but why, apart from AAF, did I, for so long, fail to offer even a quiver of resistance?

During a day out, I took my mother to Westminster Roman Catholic Cathedral. She slowly looked up and around the vast, beautiful interior and whispered:

"So big - so - so certain, it almost makes you believe it must be true."

In its paltry way, thus it is with Hudism. So - so persistent - so certain that, etc., especially when inculcated, heartily, into children.

And I'm not coming back next week at 11 a.m. for more therapy.

That's my rationale and I'm stuck with it.

By Definition - Which?

Peter Gelb, former manager of Horowitz, has openly wondered if Vladimir H was not just eccentric but also plainly crazy.

Some of the samples now quoted - just a few, not to strain credulity - may appear to lean towards a diagnosis of functional mental instability in the case of the Hudi. This, encompassing an entire identifiable group, would be a new (I think) analyst's classification: folie à famille.

Examples? Here are just a few.

A Measured View

Right from the start, if anything I wrote was criticized by a producer to the extent that some rewriting was held to be necessary, my father, a tailor and a good one, bristled:

"All I know is, I measure someone for a suit, make it,

he tries it on, it fits. So: you write it, they make a film of it. I don't recut. Why do you rewrite?"

Based on 'Movie-Making By Tape Measure', this uncritical worship of my efforts was extended by Jack to my brother Michael. He wrote a heartfelt book about jazz and received a letter from a publisher. My father carried this in his wallet, proudly, to show to friends.

It was a pro-forma letter of rejection.

I'm still at a loss to understand what he was trying to prove. The stupidity of the publisher? Michael Hudis's link with an important person? What? This incident smacks of the 'lawyer' in India who, allegedly, hung a sign at his office:

"B.A. Oxon., Failed".

Illusion

What a Hudis would dearly love to be the case, is.

Consider the growth of Nazi power. Response - repeat, to each threat:

"Britain will never allow it. Stands to reason."

This was, especially, my father's comforting mantra.

The West, including Britain, allowed German

rearmament and occupation of the Rhineland, Austria and Czechoslovakia, despite Dad's confidence. When war finally began against the Nazis, Jack said, patiently:

"What did I tell you ...?"

Taste

What a Hudis likes is automatically, nay, as if by divine revelation, not just The Best but The Only.

"Faust is The Only Opera."

"Herbert von Karajan is The Only Conductor."

"Bernard Levin is The Only Theatre Critic."

"Beethoven is The Only Symphonic Composer."

Admittedly I was a mere, trusting child at the time, but I did imbibe the conviction that, in the whole world, only - repeat only - the Hudises liked classical music. Then I heard a bit of a concert on the radio and wondered, who are all these people clapping - more aunts and uncles?

Disbelieve this if you will. That won't erase the eerie memory for me. And the Hudisian response was not to correct this lunatic fantasy, but to comment:

"What an observant boy!"

Be Whatever You Want, Little Man

I once heard an aunt declare that Gilbert and Sullivan operettas were "so nice for the kiddies". Acquiescent in all other Hudistic assumptions though I was at that time, there was, in me, a saving flicker of rebellion: I resented being thought of as a kiddie and avoided G&S for a long time. And I also assumed, nauseatingly, 'adult' attitudes whenever I could.

This unctuous pose led to my sister Sylvia saying, recently:

"You know, Norman, you were never a child."

Thanks, gang.

And, much longer ago, at Betts Street Elementary School, Stepney, sent on an errand, the four-eyed little, un-kiddy Hudisian prick that I was, airily accosted the headmaster with:

"Ah - just the man I want to see."

General Delusion

There were four Hudis brothers. All served in the Middlesex Regiment, in France, WW1. From training at Reading, my father sent home a photograph of himself in uniform. The top of his peaked cap was enclosed in an elasticated material, for rain protection.

"Look at that," said his unsurprised sister. "They've made Jack a General."

She had several cats, in succession, all named Timmy. All were, naturally, remarkable, but none so rare as Timmy IX who, when his pleas to be let out into the garden were, rarely, ignored, entered the lavatory and leapt up onto the seat.

"No shit," said writer Milton Gelman, in Hollywood, courteously, on being told about The Only Cat.

The Memo Man

Uncle Civil Servant was perhaps the most shuddering example of the Hudis conception of wit. Which is, in one word - sneer - and, when done Hudis-style, 'twere mandatory 'twere done hurtfully, implying incompetence, inability and shame thereof.

He once showed me a mock memo he'd circulated in his department, in professedly 'satiric' bureaucratic style but entirely lacking in detachment and overlaid with a creamy stratum of smiling self-satisfaction.

He did not, so far as I can tell, ever send a memo to himself, to remind him that he had some responsibility toward his brothers. When my father was felled out of any future employment by coronary thrombosis, Uncle Whitehall telephoned me with two priorities - condolence and:

"You'd better not get ill, Norman. Who'd support Jack then?"

Mr Memo trumpeted another superiority:

"I am a selective television viewer."

This set him apart from the mindless millions who switched on the TV in early evening and left it on. He demonstrated his cultural eminence ostentatiously: leaping up and switching off the TV set when a suitable programme ended, and not switching it on again until the next acceptable offering was due on screen, be the gap only a half-hour.

As justice, famously, not only has to be done but must also be seen to be done, so this elevated attitude towards television was not only announced, it was also seen being applied - an essential proviso in Hudism.

His wife, a sophisticate and intellectual, described her

life with him as "60 years of servitude".

Don't Ever Tell Hudises Anything - They Already Know

A cousin, offered a job as a typist, came to the family's one stenographer for a quick course on the machine. In the first minute, the aunt pointed to (say) the shift key, but, before she could utter a tutorial word, the cousin cut in:

"Don't tell me, Auntie. I know!"

Instead of telling her to shut up and take notes, the aunt, one Hudis to another, cosily complimented her because this little exchange illustrated one of the most highly prized dogmas of Hudism:

A Hudis never has to be taught anything. We know. A hint, perhaps, is permissible but is the equivalent of five years at university in the appropriate course topped by an honours degree. In short, we already know.

Mr Music

My dad's Brother No. 2, the Teacher, was the most

prized example of Hudisian omniscience.

The Hindus had their Untouchables?

We go one much better. We have our Unteachables. He was the supreme one - taught himself to play both violin and piano.

I remember him, nevertheless, not tossing off Mozart sonatas ("he never learned, you know") as easily as other people hum 'Three Blind Mice' (probably off-key, not being Hudi) but wearing that tolerant, distant smile of superiority in all things. That encompassed everything Hudistic, and no one had to teach him that, either. It was there. From birth. Like the umbilical cord. Only not removable.

The Good Side

Here, to the imagined accompaniment of uplifting oratorio music, I am at pains to temper all of this.

Chalk up this gesture as patronizing and, with a thousand weaknesses bedevilling me, let's ask again: who the hell am I to judge? Nevertheless, I must aim at some balance: because, though dubbed, as appropriate, Joke or Baleful, the principal Hudi each displayed, midst all the hair-raising posturing, these qualities:

Aunt Cat-Lover has already been gratefully acknowledged for Being There When It Mattered.

Uncle Teacher was superb at his job, understood the young, and this was reflected in his dealings with his daughters, nieces and nephews. He always seemed, to me, to be quietly thankful that Fate (and his intimidating father) had permitted him to do what he loved, without fanfare. This didn't prevent him from proclaiming an all-too-typical Hudistic belief that a) the Alvis was the best car ever manufactured, and b) his particular Alvis was the best of the entire output.

Uncle Civil Servant was the only Hudis who declined to join in the Hallelujah Chorus of unstinted praise for my writing. What prevented him from joining in the routine Hudisian tribute to offspring who knew, by divination, where the shift key was? Common sense, I guess, gleaned from his wife who always considered my stuff with the same careful judgement she gave to all writers, etc. I was outraged at the time, as if, in some way, betrayed, but some timorous quirk in me knew that that was what I needed and would find nowhere else within the Citadel of Hudis.

He was also top rank at his work and received the MBE for wartime services.

Uncle Estate Agent I rarely met and I therefore didn't know him to any degree.

THE OTHER
FAMILY

The Reubens of Christian Street

- which, I swear, is where my mother's family lived.

In one drastic action, the Reuben matriarch, Sura, countered, without even knowing them at the time, the Hudis's claim to infallibility in all things, and culpability in none.

One of her sons "got into bad company".

She sewed her life savings - a few golden sovereigns - into the lining of his overcoat and, at barely 14, put him on a ship for New York (where he did well).

A less Hudisian action simply cannot be imagined, because it combined clarity with resolve.

Sura's unworldly Orthodox husband, Avrohom, earned little from his modest front-room Yiddish Lending Library (Die Drei Musketeeren? Der Paperen fun Pickwick? Konig Henry der Funf?) and the meticulous penning of sacred scrolls. Sura, adoring him, kept the large family afloat.

From her, I must deduce, my mother Polly (Bela) absorbed an unyielding passion for security. She was the perfect match, therefore, for Jack. Follow the trail, repeatedly travelled:

Job offer comes along. Jack enthuses, fantasizes. Polly quivers with apprehension. What if it goes wrong? He's doing all right as he is. Why risk it all by changing?

Horses in mid-stream and frying pans and fires figure vividly in her pleas as warm discussion ensues, conclusion foregone:

Jack capitulates.

How could he, burner of steerage tickets to dry Mama's tears, fail to allay his wife's fears?

How she ever agreed to the enormous Glasgow move is a mystery. Anyway, that was a unique surrender and, to her credit, she never cited it as an example of how Reubenian catastrophe lurks within the Hudisian Aladdin's Cave of Change.

But, at all other times, it was a ritual, serving the fundamental needs of both: she maintaining the 'secure' status quo; he being 'persuaded' out of his pose of pioneer/adventurer to emerge, shiny, heroic, abandoning a course he actually feared to take as much as she did.

As Jack, in spite of unchangeable Hudis illusions, was, fundamentally, a good dad, so Polly could not be in the least faulted as a good mum.

She was not so strong as her own stoic mother, Sura. Polly never said, "Enough", when she should have, if she'd had the smallest inclination to practise Tough Love.

When the 'normal' limits of responsibility had long been crossed, when a (grown) child's vagaries had to be left to work themselves out, when hard beds self-made had to be lied upon, Polly could never detach herself for the greater good. Invariably she chose - no, choice was not a factor: her reaction was Pavlovian - ride to the rescue through hail and fog.

Is this uncrackable family fusion a specifically Jewish trait?

Yes, because I have encountered it so many times.

No, because Cockneys, Italians and Irish (to select only three groups) appear, to me, to be similarly warmly bound, especially towards the mums. And I don't doubt that they suffer the consequences of unlimited indulgence, and bend and break under the weight of burdens they should not voluntarily assume, but, in a word, do.

Also, since no generalization should ever be permitted, there have to be Jewish families (like Sura's, for God's sake) where harmful spoliation is not the norm.

Anyway, ally the probable group trait with Hudism, and the ferocious consequences are not hard to imagine.

They loved each other, did Pollyjack, but what Jack needed, in cold calculation, was a businesslike woman who could give him the illusion of his mastery while, of course, running the show and making the moves. I knew such women, especially in Hollywood: such a lady would have total charge of finances and periodically announce to well-earning husband: "Okay. Today we bought another building on Wilshire Boulevard."

On a more domestic note: Polly, using Turban Mixture, made hundreds of fruitcakes.

Of which, perhaps, the nuttiest was, arguably, me.

Editorial staff meeting,
AIR FORCE NEWS,
Ministry of Information,
Cairo. (Norman Hudis
extreme right.)

Jack

At Pinewood Studios
"An evening with Norman Hudis."
He signs for a "Carry On" fan

Norman and Rita - Hollywood garden party

Polly, Jack and Kevin

First year in Hollywood - with
Zsa Zsa Begorrah

Working on "Carry on
something - forget which one

With producer Steve Walsh

Air HQ Western Desert -
on Group Captain O'Sullivan's staff

Discussing Comedy on a
panel at the Indianapolis
Heartland film festival
(winner for "A Monkey's Tale")

Grandma Polly with young Kevin

Arty photo on promotion
to lofty rank of corporal (Unpaid)

Checking first print run of
AIR FORCE NEWS, CAIRO.
Not yet promoted to corporal...

Rita (right), her first day in
operating theatre

Stephen Hudis -
has he been here before?

Air Force News staff on the balcony of our office at the Ministry of Information, Cairo

Left to Right: George Simpson (editor):Me: Jimmy Bayes: "Gillie" Potter.
Leaning over the rail is Peter Brunswick.

Building at the back is the English Cathedral. Right behind are the palm-trees lining the River Nile

Nurse Rita Robinson, Princess Beatrice Hospital London, S.W. - 1952

80-a-day (then)

Rita

Carrying On! Director, Writer, Producer

Polly

CARRY ON STEVE! - in a blaze of glory.
Stuntman Steve Hudis, son of scriptwriter
Norman at the peak of his world record bus jump
over 15 motorcycles and flames. 108 feet.
January 12, 2000 - a Guiness book of records entry

Kevin can write just as well as
Dad - and sport a hat

Rita - nothing if not thoughtful

Rita

Grand-dad with Baby Stephen

Dad Hudis - Isaac known as
Jack, affirming "Britain will never allow it"

Sister Sylvia in the WAAF

My Mum Polly - "why don't you write as a hobby?"

Norman Hudis at the show-off wall-display of awards

The RAF's Hawkeye Hudis,
Terror of the Sinai, on guard,
Middle East, 1942

Norman Hudis in full flood

Norman

Norman and Rita taking a break from
work in England

Polly

Rita

First night of unexpected hit: Norman
Hudis (center) and Marc Sinden
(creator and producer), with
actresses Tracey Childs, Rula Lenska,
Susan Penhaligon and Eva Pope:
all of SEVEN DEADLY SINS
AND FOUR DEADLY SINNERS,
after the premiere at Hunstanton

SUBSTITUTE FAMILIES

This Feller Frood

My favourite aunt relished overhearing, on a bus, one earnest person informing another:

"There's this feller Frood, see, and he wrote a book."

An influential feller indeed, whose theories tempt many an amateur psychiatrist into solemn self-analysis. Like this:

Unconsciously (of course), I now see that I sought, in succession, steady, secure substitute families to replace my unstable one.

This belief is supported, I think, by the slightly alarming fact that it soon appeared to me that the Hudi were *playing* at being a family. In fact, as my instinct for drama grew, I thought of them as always tracked by a camera, with a microphone overhead, and appearing in an endless documentary about themselves.

Sigmund Frood may not have expressed it thus, though it seems likely he addressed the issue somewhere or other, but that's what I felt, and still feel.

So meet my life-saving other families.

1st: Newspaperman

Scribbling since I can't remember when, I vaguely saw myself as a playwright. As always, I received different and equally misleading responses from:

* Dad: as glumly reported, every word I wrote was inspired and beyond improvement.

* Mum: be secure, learn a trade, get paid every Friday, write only as a nice hobby.

Well into my working life, Polly treated my stuff as if it were an extra-curricular achievement at school, and me as a forgivably precocious child. No other explanation offers itself as to why she shyly urged a neighbour to watch *The Powder Magazine* on BBC TV when I was in my early thirties:

"Norman's written a little play."

Alarmingly, I had not moved on, in her eyes, from being the insufferably bright lad who wrote (say) a five-minutes "little play" for his kindergarten. The BBC was just a bigger classroom and a few million viewers merely another bunch of admiring parents, tolerant of errors and lavish with applause and head-pats.

For me, the Fleet Street film *This Man is News* (Barry

K. Barnes and Valerie Hobson) pointed the way forward, all Mum's terrors about shabby, heavy-drinking reporters thrust aside. I would be a newspaperman and enjoy the instant gratification of seeing what I wrote in print.

This ambition set, Napoleon would have asked: "Is he lucky?"

Incredibly. Despite an appalling academic record, my headmaster must have exercised leniency in favour of a promise, in me, perceptible but of course not anywhere near developed yet, and recommended me to the local newspaper editor. He had no vacancy but, again, must have been sufficiently intrigued to pass the recommendation on to an editor a suburb or two away.

September 1938, aged 16. First job. On a real newspaper - the still-respected *Hampstead & Highgate Express*. (I must record that a rival print offered a regular news column entitled 'Golders Green Spangles and Garden Suburb Gems'.)

Substitute Family No. 1. Whether I was collecting cricket scores on Monday morning or reviewing local dramatics, I was one of a family that made sense, and was offered protection, excitement, variety, correction, with the constant unspoken acceptance that I wanted to belong to the real, normal world as a result of observing it coolly at close quarters.

To this day, the ambience of a newspaper's editorial room stirs me to the sharp nostalgia of returning to a long-left home (though it lacks the urgent clatter of typewriters).

When war came, I was issued with a white steel helmet marked 'PRESS'. This was like being admitted to adulthood in a united family, with no illusions about its place in the scheme of things or the disproportionate importance of one of its sons.

2nd: Airman

You may never get near an aeroplane (sorry: aircraft) in the RAF, but you are always referred to as an Airman. At least that's the way it was in my five-and-a-half years' WWII service. I joined on 27 July 1940, my 18th birthday, and was accepted as fit to become what I volunteered for: Air Gunner. My one good eye, at the medical, was apparently judged to be well up to the task.

Battle of Britain effectively looming, I expected, on enlistment, to be rushed immediately to an hour or so's gunnery tuition and, the next day, after sewing the winged letters 'AG' to my tunic, I'd be up there in London's threatened skies, polishing off the Luftwaffe one by one, thus emulating Air Gunner Sgt Hannah VC, 18, for eight shillings and threepence a day.

Instead I was sent for Basic Training, medically examined rather more stringently and pronounced not only unfit (vision) to fly but, implicitly, considered a menace to any crew I might have joined. So they 're-mustered' me, deeply downcast, as an ACH/GD: Aircrafthand/General Duties.

In that capacity I worked as telephone operator, engine-cannibalizing, armed escort on train and road journeys, cookhouse, clerk et al. - and I mean al. - in England and the Middle East.

In every way, the RAF was my substitute family No. 2 and, despite some ritual rankers' moaning, I gladly gave it all my love. And still do.

The central action, which clinched the RAF in its

familial role for me, is the saga of the sergeants (cast, easily, as big brothers) who saved the baby 55 RSU from being abandoned in the desert, thus giving me the crucial clue to the style and role of sergeants for That Film.

Memories - just a few ...

Called to Church Parade, I asked the Sergeant if, as a Jew, I had to attend: "Ee no. Tha'd better fook off else get in trooble with bloody rabbi."

Asked for his Service number, another stated, kindly:

"Haven't one. When I joined up we all knew each other."

"When was that, Sarge?"

"When Pontius was a Pilate."

In 1940 England, we were issued rifles and placed on guard. Our instructions: anyone approaches, call out: "Halt who goes there?" No reply? Say the same again. Still no response? Warn: "Halt or I fire."

"And if the suspicious one doesn't halt, what do we do then, Sarge?"

"Fook all. We got no bloody bullets."

Why I didn't use these golden lines, in some form, in the script, I can't, at this distance, begin to imagine. Or, for that hysterical matter, the occasion when, in the blackout it's true, I smartly saluted a uniformed Blackpool tram conductor, in the firm and respectful belief that he was a Polish Flight Lieutenant.

And let a doughty, phlegmatic sergeant, substitute as rallying big brother, typically have the last word on the troopships.

It is firmly believed that, spotting a green-faced airman leaning against a corridor wall as the vessel heaved, he kindly tended him thus:

"Outside, son. You want to be sick. No shame in that. No honour in fighting it. Out with it, every drop. Over the side. But keep your eyes open at all costs. Eventually, a small nut-brown little ring will come up. Hold on to it, son. It's your arsehole."

How about a gruff grandfather figure? The outwardly intimidating Group Captain Garth Richard O'Sullivan, who still wore the pilot's wings of the RFC (Royal Flying Corps) from WWI. He ultimately proved to have, if not a heart of gold, at least a recognizable heart when it was, rarely, for fear of spoiling the beneficiary, let out for an airing. I clerked for him at HQ Western Desert, during the final push, which began at El Alamein and finished, for me, at Ben Gardane, Tunisia.

I'd always yearned for the impossible: a 20-year-old, with barely two years' experience on a weekly newspaper, somehow getting into RAF Public Relations. Mentioning this to one sergeant, I got the encouraging reply:

"That can be managed - if you know Winston Churchill."

I remembered this when, suddenly, the group captain summoned me to his jeep and we went to a parade on the sand - thousands of servicemen. We were a little late and so had to park at the front - within touching distance of Winston Churchill's arrival. He thanked us for defeating the Axis in this area.

Now give this a Ripley: believe or no. Maybe it was because I, hair-raisingly, to think of it now, stood up to GCOS in a couple of grammatical instances, like what constitutes a split infinitive. Whatever the reason, when Middle East RAF HQ announced the publication of a weekly newspaper, this edgy senior officer summoned me brusquely and dictated, to Command Public Relations, a wildly exaggerated summary of my wunderkind journalistic capabilities.

It worked, and, the night before I left Desert HQ, we were machine-gunned by a last-ditch marauding German fighter. This was only the second time in my experience: altogether I had a much safer war than Londoners.

And so to Garden City, Cairo, to join the editorial staff of the *Air Force News*. Having begun to learn my trade in a London suburb, I was suddenly on the staff of a publication serving an area one-and-a-half times the size of the United States.

And it was growing, as Middle East RAF units penetrated Europe, and *AFN* was flown to them even unto the borders of the English Channel.

And I visited most of it, harvesting a crop of imperishable memories: especially that of the RAF Commander Paiforce (Persia and Iraq), showing visible signs of gobsmacking when he was interviewed by a non-commisssioned type. But he was an officer and a gentleman and behaved nicely, as did 1270676 Corporal (Acting, Unpaid) Hudis.

Some time later, a breathless Cpl Hammond, who ran the *AFN* admin office, entered the editorial room, stammering:

"Cpl Hudis - there's a Group Captain O'Sullivan to see you ...!"

There he was, on the landing, leaning on his reluctantly employed walking stick. Poking me in the ribs with it, he snapped:

"Well, Hudis - Editor of *The Times* yet? Don't let me down now, or I'll have your guts for garters."

Without letting me reply, he turned sharply and left.

Moral: gruff grandpas do what has to be done, and see that it is taking effect and appreciated. Then, gruffer than ever, dismissing thanks, move on.

The RAF was the best and warmest of my substitute families.

3rd: Publicity Man (well, perhaps only 2½)

The substitute family parallel weakens somewhat when applied to the next phase: post-war Publicity

Representative for the J. Arthur Rank Organisation.

But, to the extent that all of us, working then for the vast Rank and Korda companies, aimed at putting British films on the world map, we were a family of sorts, though a necessarily competitive one.

I began, in London, based at an office about 100 yards from Piccadilly Circus, as a 'picture plugger'. Aim: to persuade magazines, ranging from *The Tatler* (upper-crust) to *Everybody's Weekly* (mass-market) to print stills relating to Rank Organisation productions and, of course, to credit the titles of said movies.

Then, on to where I really wanted to work: in succession, Islington, Denham and Pinewood Studios. Now I was a Unit Publicity Representative, responsible for gathering suitable publicity material to promote the film in question on its release.

I stayed too long in publicity (seven years at Pinewood alone) simply, lazily, because it was fun - and a quite well-paid apprenticeship in film production.

Then I got the urge to write a play.

4th: Writers

Sensibly, for once, and instinctively (all right, Napoleon - luckily) following the sage advice to all literary aspirants, "Write what you know", the play *Here is The News* was set in a newspaper office.

The publicity man in me persisted: I was pleased with the reflection that four or five times a day, on BBC Radio, the title of my drama was given a free plug.

Produced by the Under-30 Theatre Group at Leatherhead, Surrey, the cast included Michael Blakemore, now a top stage director in London and New York.

It also got a showing at Lucille Lortel's White Barn Theatre, Connecticut, where a reviewer found it "rather uncompelling theatre".

I'm very much inclined to agree, but that didn't deter Pinewood's Executive Producer, Earl St John, from giving me a contract as a screenwriter.

Earl provided a nice link to the beginning of my journey as a writer: he was the producer of the film, for Paramount British, which urged me into becoming a newspaper reporter - 'This Man is News'. The amiable

American had a strong history himself.

He came to Europe in WWI with the Texas Motor-Cycle Regiment and stayed on to become manager of the Tivoli Cinema in the Strand. There, he made *Wings* into a bigger attraction than it already was, by expanding the screen for the aerial dogfight sequences. Then on to Paramount and, finally, Pinewood.

Since that contract, I've been in the family of writers for big and small screen, as a member of the Writers' Guilds of Great Britain, America, Australia and Canada, and Picket Captain during the 1988 strike, at CBS studios, Hollywood. Suffice to say, holding back emotion, that this family consists of healthy and open competitors, instantly rallying as supportive when common interests are threatened.

I can't express fervently enough my gratitude to my dear substitute families; and hope that they never found me an unsatisfactory son.

MY REAL FAMILY

Four Months - 50 Years

33 Eccleston Square, London SW1. I shared 4th-floor Flat D (no lift) with actor Robert Brown, who appeared with Roger Moore in many Bond films.

It was there that I threw a party after the telecast of *The Powder Magazine*. As an augur of my fairly ruinous concept of relative values, it was ominous: I was paid £75 by the BBC and spent £40 on the party.

Around the corner, the redoubtable butcher Ted Stepney served us well; and his wife Madge, a former nurse and fascinated by The Biz, adored us. To cut a short story even shorter, she asked me to help with sketches, parodies and the like for a Christmas show she was putting on for the patients together with some of her former colleagues at the Princess Beatrice Hospital.

There, at rehearsal, she tap-danced, with swirling umbrella and the unbearably pretty Nurse Rita Robinson, to 'Singin' in the Rain'. Two memorable events, equally drastic, occurred within minutes: a piece of scenery fell on Ms Robinson's shoulder; and I fell for that shoulder and everything attached. Four months later we married. I did warn that this was, in essence, a very short story.

It is extremely doubtful if anyone has ever existed less Hudisian than Marguerita Frances Hudis (née Robinson) of Portadown, Northern Ireland, then Croydon and a joyous room at 37 Earls Court Square. How I won her against the intense competition of a flock of young doctors, I've no idea - especially as, later and with nice judgement, her beauty was such that Milton Gelman dubbed her Zsa Zsa Begorrah.

The inheritance of Hudism is not, as I have hinted, easy to shake off. After 50 years of marriage to a steady but, when necessary, fearless and fiery temperament like Rita's, I still don't claim to be free of lingering Pollyjack effects.

I know that, terrified at fatherhood, I have not always well served our sons, Stephen and Kevin, but have many times applied fleeting, recognizable Hudis demands (perfectibility, for one). They do not seem to hold these occasions against me, which is heartening: it argues that the Hudis gene may have skipped this generation and that, on the whole, I have tried at least to boot it along out of range. One hopes it has left unmarked the two most glowingly beautiful grandchildren, Veronica and Cameron, from Steve's marriage to one of Tennessee's loveliest exports, novelist Lindy.

The sons can, I believe, be soberly characterized in simple contrast:

One, Stephen was incurably bitten by The Biz Bug.

The younger very early swatted the deadly insect flat.

The older first.

Stephen

always wanted to be a performer. When still a very polite English eight-year-old, he asked *Lucy* writer Bob O'Brien:

"Excuse me, sir, do you have any vacancies for child actors?"

With the aid of agent Toni Kelman (prize client, Jodie Foster), he began with a bang - directed by Steven Spielberg (who called him "a thinking actor") in a segment of *The Psychiatrist*, entitled 'The Private World of Martin Dalton'. Many roles followed, culminating in that of Charlie Schwartz in *The Cowboys*, starring John

Wayne.

Realistically, few child actors smoothly segue as performers into maturity. Reactions to the sudden plunge, in late teens, from desirability to anonymity range from prolonged desolation to, more rarely, sensible calm adjustment to the plain fact of drastic change.

Stephen? Perhaps from his tough great-grandma, Sura Reuben, he inherited a strong core of realism, consisting of sober acknowledgment of a difficult situation, and the resolve not to succumb to it.

From the other strand of his heredity, there is no sign of what Hemingway called "the deep Irish love of defeat". If I placed any credence in astrology, I'd say that he is a super Taurus - stubborn and dedicated. He has become a noted stunt co-ordinator and 2nd Unit director. He is also a very credible writer, with a stage play about Kent State and a screenplay on young drug addiction -two powerful works, awaiting their chances.

On 12 January 2000, he drove a bus up a ramp and across a line of 15 motorcycles, while flames leapt up higher than the bus roof. The feat is in the *Guinness*

Book as a World Record.

I like to meditate that, whatever else is ever said about Stephen Robin Hudis, no one will ever be able to comment that, for want of trying, he missed the bus.

I did, once. And if I'd caught it, Stephen and Kevin would never have been born.

Numbers of people have said, merely by looking at him, that Stephen "has been here before." At once I have to say that while I respect all beliefs, I cannot offer more than a polite nod to reincarnation. Nevertheless:

During my time on the Air Force News, I went on a training flight of RAF crews converting from twin-engined aircraft to American four-engined bombers. This followed a prescribed navigational course to drop "bombs" (photos of targets) and return to base in Palestine. (And the censor followed his prescribed path and cut my account from four columns to three lines.)

I was assigned to aircraft (say) A for Arthur.

Rather a peculiar sight, with goggles over my RAF steel-rimmed glasses, and a parachute dangling ungracefully – the very model for a movie called "The Incredible Expanding Insect" – I reported to the Ops

Room. Checking on A for Arthur, I chanced upon a familiar name on the blackboard as the captain of another crew. A glance around and the family resemblance was unmistakeable.

Approached, the brother of my former RSU CO at once asked me to fly with him. It would give his brother a big kick. I agreed and sought out A for Arthur's captain to explain the change.

He was one of the most handsome young men I have ever seen. Blond, blue-eyed – the entire vigorous young male prototype. He readily agreed to my change of aircraft.

The flight was uneventful except for the predictable mishap that my oxygen mask slipped off and I became somewhat light-headed. We also strayed slightly over the Turkish border and were desultorily fired upon. To which, in a lilting South African accent, our captain said "Captain to crew. Fuck this" and, "bombs" accurately delivered, turned for greater altitude, and home.

To learn that A for Arthur had slammed into a hillside near Beirut, with the loss of all aboard.

From one airbase, in the Levant, in war, to another in

California, where "Peace Is Our Profession" was not only the blazoned motto of the US Air Force, but the title of a two-part "Lassie" show, guest-starring Stephen Hudis.

The airmen offered the 10-year-old boy the chance to sit at the controls of an aircraft. What boy would not leap at the opportunity?

When they began to explain the controls etc., he, politely (unlike his distant Hudisian relative, Miss Shift Key) forestalled them. He knew what they were all for.

Stephen Hudis was then blond, and is still blue-eyed and extremely handsome, like the young, doomed captain of A for Arthur

All This and Kevin Too

Kevin briefly aped Stephen and got a few roles. There came the day, though, when he had to stand on a bench in the back row of a whole crowd of kids, wave his arms and yell some ad slogan. This happened a couple of times, and then he jumped down and said to Rita, "This is stupid", and they went home.

We've seen a few distressing situations where stage-mothers undergo withdrawal symptoms when the equally bewildered boy or girl hits a bad patch or fades out of employment entirely. The descent from being 'special' and cosseted to ordinary life frequently causes bewilderment in the child, and agonies of deprivation in the mother. Would that so many of these in the past and to come would cut clean from The Biz as early and as simply as did Kevin Franklin Hudis, who declares today:

"If it turns and burns, I'll drive it."

In positive detail, this means he's hauled transporter-loads of cars all over the USA; driven for movies (including *The Fast and the Furious*) and TV; and been on emergency call to rescue stranded drivers and vehicles on and off the highway for the American Automobile Association. He combines a capacity for contentment with healthy bursts of impatience with inefficiency and stupidity. This, obviously, is a lingering trace of Hudism - but, critically, in his thrice-blessed case, he is controlled and rational.

FROM PINE
TO HOLLY

It Began With Auntie Ada

Not my true Aunt, but firm friend of a real one, the only 120% hypochondriac I ever met. Her death spawned an early NH line: "She has come to the end of her long and valiant struggle against health."

Her friend Ada was altogether livelier. She gave me her American film-fan magazines and, to my fascinated movie conception of New York as a vibrating paradise for boys practising piano to become Gershwins, there was now added a gleaming imagery of Hollywood.

Skip years and years on to my office at No. 6, The Byeway, Rickmansworth, Herts.

There I took the crucial phone call.

"This is Lee Rosenberg. I'm a Hollywood literary agent and ... etc."

It was no prank. Lee was indeed the Rosenberg of Adams, Ray and Rosenberg. Their interest in me sprang from the freak US success of *Carry On Nurse*, and I agreed to their representing me in the States.

But nothing happened. The weeks of my stalled contract with Peter Rogers were racing past. Paid but not employed in the UK, I decided to go to Hollywood and meet with AR&R, literary agents, of Sunset Boulevard.

Peter Rogers only required that I should not use the phrase 'Carry On' in the title of anything I wrote there. (Later he copyrighted the phrase.)

Oh Nurse!

Four jobs, all pilot scripts (= samples for series) came about as a result of intensive interviews, four or more a day, at the major studios.

Oh Nurse, my own concept, was, predictably enough, the most attractive of the scripts, even given that I knew little of American hospital life and did scant research. Four production companies competed for it.

Among them was Bob Hope's. His offer alone included a guarantee that the show would be aired and that he would appear in it, at least in the pilot.

I don't know if this offer merited description as 'fabulous' but, lost for other words, it certainly sounded magical to me.

It might have led anywhere.

Why did I turn it down?

Because Hope's team of fabled writers would have worked on the script. My name would be among theirs in the credits. All this, plus Hope's appearance, perhaps as walk-on anchorman, would wrenchingly change the nature of the story and I'd lose the sole writing credit.

I was sweltering in a phone booth when Sam Adams, Rick Ray and Lee Rosenberg, on a conference call, urgently requested that I decide what I wanted to do.

I went with Four Star, where my immediate contact was Nina Laemmle, an Englishwoman who'd married into the legendary family whose patriarch, Carl, founded Universal Pictures.

One network, during early negotiations, provided a breathless earlier moment.

"I take it," said their representative, "that you want to produce the show?" This, routine in America, contrasts so starkly as to be painful with the prevailing attitude in England at that time.

It has, thankfully, changed since and British writers tend to get their due as producers as well.

Oh Nurse! read well and I was called back the next

year to do revisions. The Network's Perry Lafferty was reliably reported to me as liking the show, but could not persuade a majority to buy it.

"Guaranteed airing" echoed the honeyed voice of Bob Hope as *Oh Nurse!* died on the vine ...

"I take it," the network man might just as well have said, "you want to sabotage your own show by turning down Bob Hope?"

The Move

Family holiday plans went awry.

"Los Angeles instead?" I asked Rita.

With ten-month-old Kevin, and Stephen aged eight, it was off to Hollywood and, for me at any rate, with no intention of returning. AR&R began to get work for me from the day of our arrival.

My fundamental fault, from that moment on? A sadly familiar one in Hollywood: to believe that 'the good times' would go on for ever.

Good they were.

U.N.C.L.E.

The first series on which I had some Hollywood success was MGM-based *The Man From U.N.C.L.E.*, the jazzy brainchild of Englishman Norman Felton, with one character, Napoleon Solo, borrowed from Ian Fleming.

Executive Producer Boris Ingster was a rather conventionally colourful Russian. Let *U.N.C.L.E.*'s Assistant Director Eddie Saeta contribute a fitting moment, which arose when Boris called an after-hours meeting of department heads at a moment's notice, because he'd had "a revolutionary idea".

Discussion began at 6 p.m. and Boris flamboyantly ordered in a great feast to sustain the participants. Supper was taken without pause in the proceedings, at 10 p.m. All was settled by 2 a.m. As the weary departed, Eddie said:

"Sorry to eat and run, Boris."

When Boris left the show, he threw a huge party for us, launched and continued sailing on Dom Perignon. It was almost his last typical flourish. Not long afterwards, he died. Heart.

U.N.C.L.E. Producer David Victor, also Russian,

originally wrote radio scripts which can still be heard on some college stations, went on to TV, set his sights on becoming a producer and doggedly became one.

He was not one to discuss scripts line by line: broad comments, quickly delivered, judgement while you wait. He was the one producer, in my experience, who rarely stayed in the studio a tick beyond 6 p.m., when his wife Florence arrived to drive him home, and home he went. Not for him anguished late-hour rewrites and suchlike.

David invariably called me 'Norman Hudis - English Boy-Writer'. Endearing but, to me, not as much as his instinctive action at a birthday party where, pained by the cake's inscription, 'Many Happy Return's', he surreptitiously removed the extraneous apostrophe with a spoon. Was he entirely satisfied?

"No. There was no way I could then move the 's' closer to the 'n'."

His home was carefully chosen: Beverly Hills, just off that bend of Sunset Boulevard where the entrance to the University of California, Los Angeles, branches off.

He used to say, "I don't get heart attacks. I give heart

attacks."

He died while strolling The University grounds. Heart.

This Day and Ageism

Consider now, vitally, 'Ageism', a Hollywood product spread worldwide with the ease and vigour, if not the fun, of *I Love Lucy* and *The Simpsons*.

This simple guide to action possesses the deadly unarguable simplicity of The Final Solution:

"You are Russian/a Jew/Black. Die."

Substitute, in Hollywood, for all these Nazi-deemed subhumans - 'Writer, Aged 40'. That's Ageism.

At least the Nazis worked their hated groups to death with a derisive chance of survival. Hollywood firmly denied their despised target people work, because (among other sweeping slogans) "No one over 40 can write a love scene."

George Kirgo, then President of the Writers' Guild of America, mildly countered:

"Some of us have kept diaries."

Not so light-heartedly, remember that in the mid-twentieth century some Hollywood writers dyed their hair, even chest hair, so that the 'young' look could be carelessly displayed with an open-neck shirt. No one, so far as I can determine, carried the disguise down to the genital strands though, God knows, sex for work is not a rare bargain, even when one party is over 40.

Careers ended. People, dyed hair or not, suffered deeply.

The Writers' Guild did and does its formidable best to counter the persecution. Some schemes were set up but, to me, they placed the 'aged' writer ever more firmly in a separate category - ageism and apartheid in an unholy mix.

Take a pause for just one tragedy in which the writer in question underwent two good old industry blows in rapid succession.

This was Larry Forrester: Scot, vigorous writer, fertile, born storyteller. He came to Hollywood to write *Tora! Tora! Tora!*, the Pearl Harbour story. I'd best lay to rest here, my 'inJewdicious' line that the sequel would be titled *Talmud! Talmud! Talmud!*

His final *Tora* script was lauded. He relaxed. He then

learned that some more work was needed on it - and that another writer had been hired. This diluted his sole screen credit. No reason was given. Larry, ever-willing and energetic, and by then a saturated expert on Pearl Harbour, wasn't called back for this work.

Tough Glaswegian and former RAF fighter pilot Larry was his closest to sobs.

He was a fanatically hard worker. But time doesn't have to overexert itself. And with the passage of time work became elusive to over-40 Larry.

Characteristically, he became a member of the Guild Committee formed to tackle ageism. After one early meeting, he got home to Pauline and his two adopted children, collapsed, died. Heart.

The industry he loved broke it, said someone at the Memorial, in the Writers' Guild Theatre.

His was not the only death that can be attributed to ageism - a system that deems you're too old to write a love scene so you might as well be dead.

I remember Larry on other counts.

We were once on an Awards Committee of the British Writers' Guild. A name was proposed. A member objected: "But he's not English!"

Larry flared:

"I don't care if he's Chinese. He's a member of this Guild and the nomination stands."

Classic: Larry suffered a perforated ulcer when in Tokyo on *Tora* business, to meet Akira Kurosawa. He and producer Elmo Williams called at the legendary director's house. A young aide informed them that Mr Kurosawa could not see them because he was busy committing suicide.

Elmo W (veteran Hollywood): "Shall we wait or come back later?"

More of U.N.C.L.E.

On this show I met Milton Gelman, who became one of my three closest friends in Hollywood. A deeply experienced writer and serenely cynical re. the vices and vagaries of The Biz, he swept away, almost single-handedly, my illusory Hudis confusions. At first resisting his patient wisdom, I was able to learn, gradually, a more balanced view from him. An example:

When I moaned that I was a lousy father, with no idea how to deal with our children, he swept this 'modest' self-flagellation aside, brusquely:

"You did the best you knew how, in the circumstances, at the time."

No perfectionist omniscient Hudis could ever have come up with that sobering, accepting, balanced judgement.

Another example:

I'd left a script in England with a producer friend. When I asked for news of it, some time later, he'd lost it. I wrote a blistering letter to him about how writers are taken for granted and worse by the likes of him, etc., and read it to Milton on the phone.

Pause.

"Is that it?" grunted the serene man from Milwaukee. "Well, *you* feel better: mission accomplished. Now throw it away. If you send it, the guy'll be uncomfortable for three minutes, then rationalize his action to himself and never employ you again."

No bristling, blameless, smouldering, vengeful (yes, all of the above - as you have read) Hudis could ever have advised thus. In such a circumstance, your initiated member of the tribe is almost sworn to behave, obsessively and forever, like a singularly unsophisticated party in an especially ugly divorce.

Finally, he quit, to teach full-time at Loyola Marymount University.

Typically he worked far harder than necessary, especially when it came to assessing students' scripts. Ten-page closely typed comments, in astonishing detail, and carefully phrased, flowed from him, for each of 20 scripts at a time.

It needs to be reported that one other tutor there murmurously questioned the fitness of a Jew teaching at a Catholic University.

This was no surprise to realist Milton Gelman who, re. his daughter, was told by a Midwest teacher:

"No Jew-girl is ever going to graduate from my class."

He serves also as a stark example of what some writers suffered during a crucial strike, which won invaluable benefits.

He went into it abandoning $30,000-worth of work. He ended up $80,000 in debt. And his experience is by no means unique.

Flash forward: at the end of a pre-strike meeting in my era, a young Guild member passionately begged as follows:

"We can't go on strike! I've just bought a house and we are about to have a baby. We have the Pension, Health Care and Residuals. Do we even need a Guild any more?"

Milton and his early-Guild colleagues shouldered immense sacrifices - some losing their homes - in order to gain the conditions enjoyed by Hollywood and New York film and TV writers today.

It is sadly inevitable, I suppose, that at least one writer of the later 'me' generation, with no intimate acceptance of the concept of a trade union, questioned, from his sincere perspective, whether we now need a Guild at all.

A third party was rarely absent from my meetings with Milt. An imaginary screenwriter, Milton's joyous invention, Harold Shmidlap was a bland, beaming Hollywood Candide, convinced that all was for the best in the worst of impossible worlds. His considerable professional claim to fame was as the fearless creator of those innovative yet trend-conscious dramatic TV series, *Space Rabbi* and *Frontier Accountant*.

How did Harold Shmidlap manage to keep writing during ageism? Simple:

"I lied about my height."

I was in London when Milton feebly called me, from his final hospital.

"They tell me I have one-quarter of a heart left. It will have to do."

The Crux

U.N.C.L.E. was a joy. My scripts flowed quite easily.

Post-Boris, Anthony Spinner became producer and we became quite close. A writer himself, Tony dealt with improvable drafts in an exemplary manner: he was courteous and treated writers as willing colleagues, not fractious, unteachable pupils. The key to his approach:

"No one sets out to write a bad script."

Too many story editors and others behave as if a draft unsatisfactory to them was composed deliberately and in malice to make their lives miserable, and unleash negative venom in response.

Never did Anthony Spinner stoop to such self-righteous indignation, because - well worth repeating - "No one sets out to write a bad script."

Two more bonuses from knowing him: Tony does a biting impersonation of Bela Lugosi, and ad libs fitting dialogue at story conferences which the writer is well advised to write down and use.

Note also that Robert Vaughan (Napoleon Solo) was in no way offhand, and it has to be recalled that, exceptionally, David McCallum (Illya Kuryakin) never relaxed his efforts to improve scene and performance. Both characters were perfectly slotted when David Victor initially briefed me:

"Napoleon relaxes with a broad. Illya sleeps in a glass coffin."

Among those present: Telly Savalas, Curt Jurgens, Herbert Lom.

And Joan Crawford.

They cast her in a one-and-a-half-minute role. She was paid $3,000 to come back, for one day, to MGM, and spent half her fee hiring the legendary hairdresser from her great days, Sydney Guilaroff.

I was film-fan-thrilled with it all.

The day she was cast, I told Rita: "We've got Joan Crawford!"

Stephen (aged eight): "Who's he?"

I'll tell you who, son. She's the woman who, sent home by MGM for the last time, was warned by William Haines that "when you begin to lose your career in the picture business, it's like walking on nothing".

Style

Defined, literally, in my book here as Ely+Edie Landau.

Ely was physically as big as his concepts, and weathered storms as imperturbably as he relished success. Edie, on four hours' sleep a night, equalled his energy and also qualified 'in her spare time' as a lawyer so that she, in addition to being his co-producer, could save on legal fees.

I was introduced to the Landaus by Mort Abrahams, one of David Victor's 'boys' who took the producer path, very notably at 20th Century-Fox where he guided the *Planet of the Apes* movies.

Sidelight: friend actor David Watson was cast in one of them. Rita, driving through the 20th lot was hailed - "Hi Rita!" - by a monkey taking the sun outside Make-Up and Coca-Cola through a straw up one of his low ape nostrils.

Through Mort, I was hired by the Landaus to script *Arigato* (Japanese for 'thank you') from the novel by Richard Condon.

Its quirky story told of a rapscallion, strapped-for-funds British naval officer with a French wife, whose father is a none-too-scrupulous perfumier. The Brit dreams up an audacious caper to hijack a liner and dump all the cars in its hold into the sea, to make room for a consignment of stolen vintage wines, offloaded from a smaller vessel, for onward transmission to waiting, affluent buyers in Japan.

Again, writing this sophisticated script was a sheer delight. My favourite line was to be uttered by a distraught motorist as she saw her vehicle tipped into the sea:

"Jesus! Jesus! Save my Jag!"

But it was never to be uttered.

Financial backing vanished. Overnight, *Arigato* sank.

One of Ely's quirks was never to write 'The End' on a script.

Because You Never Know.

Indeed you don't.

The Doctor is In

Universal Studios, for a long stint on *Marcus Welby MD*, the creation of Executive Producer David Victor, produced by David O'Connell. I worked, in succession, with Story Editors Nina Laemmle and Earl Booth. Among the directors - the affable Leo Penn, father of Sean.

Welby, set against today's *House* and *Grey's Anatomy*, was medically bland. But during its run, applicants at US medical schools chose the calling of General Practitioner, Welby's field, in markedly increased numbers. For a while, at any rate, it looked like being a case of the doctor is in - very in. And Welby should be duly credited for its influence on that statistic.

Talking of credits: consider Connie Izay, née Buffalini

- a petite, omniscient nurse who entered The Biz in First Aid at Universal. Among her early cases: someone who'd slightly slammed his hand in a car door. She treated him and entered the details in the log, naming the patient as Eastwood, C., working in Transportation. That's How Green Was Our Connie.

I met her when she had advanced to become Nursing Adviser on the *Welby* unit. No precedent existed for her invaluable work to receive screen credit.

Connie went on to *M*A*S*H* and, despite intervention by Alan Alda, no screen credit was offered her at 20th Century-Fox either.

We had long since become friends and Rita helped the then cancer-ridden Connie during her final weeks on the show.

When she died, an episode was dedicated to her, on screen. She finally got her credit. In this case, one must sourly ask, "Was this death, applauded by Hollywood, a good career move?"

Close friends of Connie and her husband, actor-director Vic Izay, were Mary and Frank Lauria; he, a former ballad singer. Mary was also well into the music business as a lyric writer (big hit: 'Half-Breed' for Cher).

Pivotal moment in her life: she was the first woman to be offered a TV news-anchor job. "But I am an actress," she declared, refusing.

One of those shuddering decisions: had she taken the job, who knows where it would have led, as other women made names and fortunes in TV news.

Earl Booth, ex-USAF air-gunner in the Far East, and Nina were equally easy to work with. Nina left only because she tired of preoccupation with illness on *Welby*, and accepted a job as Story Editor on *Born Free*, working in Africa. Incurably, and by then, I'm afraid, predictably, I asked her to drop me a lion.

Memorable: two *Welby* episodes of mine.

'A Necessary End'. Title from *Julius Caesar*: "seeing that death, a necessary end, will come when it will come." Story of an intrepid woman news-photographer, bitten by a malevolent bug in South America. The result, evident only years later - irreversible heart damage from Chagas Disease. Anne Baxter guest-starred and told me (to Rita's mild surprise) that the script showed how much I understood women.

The script was nominated that year, by the Guild, for Best Dramatic Episode.

'Hell Is Upstairs'. Schoolgirl victim of an ailment that causes involuntary spasmodic movement, making the sufferer, usually of high intelligence, unable to attend school, among other deprivations, to say nothing of the unending strain on the parents.

We discovered that Dr Irving S. Cooper had developed a cryogenic surgical procedure to deal with the involved section of the brain. He co-operated gladly and so we were able to script and screen an extremely tense operating sequence, observed by Welby in the OR, as he comforted the conscious child-patient, and explained by Dr Kiley (James Brolin), Welby's partner, to the mother (Shirley Ann Knight) - "Sweet Jesus keep his hand steady" - in an adjoining room.

This is the only show of mine, to my knowledge, to have a known effect on a viewer, far beyond entertainment.

When it aired in Canada, some children rushed to their mother, excitedly: this show on TV's about what their brother had, and it's curable! The hard-pressed woman watched the rest of the episode and shot off a furious letter to David O'Connell, protesting that TV had no right to raise false hopes like this. Her boy had been to a dozen doctors and all diagnoses and treatments had failed (not an unusual experience with this treacherous illness). David assured her that we would not dare invent anything so cruelly misleading and put her in touch with Dr Cooper. We later learned that the boy was treated, successfully.

PS: at a party given by a doctor friend of Rita's, I found myself holding a few medics enthralled by my talk of this condition, the gleanings of not very much research for the script. They had, it seemed, barely heard of the disease, and I was asked if I practised as its specialist in England or the USA.

An episode of especial appeal to me was 'To Live Another Day' - about an illness which renders the victim, obviously extremely hazardously, oblivious to pain. It mainly affects Jews. Earl said:

"Do we change it to a Christian, or go the Oy Vay route?"

We went Oy Vay, and received one letter accusing Robert Young of bowing to Jewish pressure to bring about sympathy for the Hebes who, anyway, deserved everything they got and are yet to get, one Holocaust not being enough.

Lighter moment: not on one of my *Welby* episodes, Dorothy Lamour, the least self-important star, had to show her bare stomach. She convincingly and mischievously protested that she was not appearing in 'The Road to Gall Bladder Surgery' but, grudgingly, finally appeared to agree.

Came the day. On the operating table, under the cameras, they drew back the covering. On her navel, courtesy of the make-up department, were two winking eyelashes.

Those tense 'stat' moments when a supine emergency patient is rushed, on a trolley, out of the elevator and turns sharply into the waiting Operating Room? One such turn was so decisive that the patient, tubes and all, shot off the trolley onto the floor.

Final memory: the closing show. This involved Kiley romantically, but the girl would not abandon her exciting job, involving much travel.

The last scene led to the viewer anticipating her saying: "I get by." I changed this to get the appropriate cynical variation, "I jet by."

Sure as sin, the actress said: "I get by."

No one on the set noticed. The line was not re-shot correctly, a matter of five filming minutes, on the last day.

And so, the last line of the last scene, of the last episode, lost what little sparkle it may have radiated and was rendered needlessly banal.

The Queen and I

Having garnered awards, in his time, from Protestant, Catholic and Jewish groups, David Victor figured he'd easily obtain validation from all three denominations for a TV series of Bible stories. To introduce the show, his English boy-writer was hired to script a 90-minute *Story of Esther*.

Had it clicked, such a series might have lasted for years given that the source is inexhaustible.

But, someone up there decided that 90 minutes was

too long.

The film was cut to one hour, with a commentary read beautifully by Raymond (Perry Mason) Burr. Naturally, I bemoaned the compression of the narrative, but, for whatever reason, that was the end of the Bible series, though *Esther* was screened, and I did receive two awards and a WGA nomination.

PS - and a zinger it is. The show was rushed into production partly because another company was also filming the Esther story. So I was writing alongside production meetings, already in progress, and was furnished, daily, with sequence sheets in which the action of each scheduled scene was very briefly described.

One such précis, pure workmanlike Hollywood, gleams across the decades:

"Esther lays King."

It Takes a Thief

Universal continued.

Director Barry Shear, a supporter since we met on *U.N.C.L.E.*, recommended me to Paul Mason, producing *It Takes a Thief*. (The astonishingly inventive Glen Larson, who could write a script in a few hours if rock music was played loud enough to him during the process, produced for this show too.) Robert Wagner starred, urbanely, as an ex-criminal working, at Bondian-level jet-set elegance, as a globe-trotting agent for the 'SIA'.

In one of my episodes, Al Mundy (Wagner), blood-loss-wounded and in further peril, wanders the streets in delirium, meeting nothing but betrayal. A central scene during this 'Odd Man Out' journey had him hallucinating being questioned by a psychiatrist.

Joseph Cotten (Mundy's boss in the series) showed the script to an analyst he knew, who pronounced the scene an extraordinarily credible portrayal of the mind and character of a clandestine agent. Well done, NH.

Barry, ever alert to create memorable effects, 'improved' the scene during editing, by distorting the soundtrack. Perfectly legitimate as a means of enabling the viewer to share the aural experience of an individual under such stress - but at the cost of rendering the crucial and expertly validated dialogue inaudible?

Paul Mason hired me to script a movie that was finally titled *The Hong Kong Wink*. Barry was to direct. Later Paul assigned me to an episode of *C.H.I.P.S.* back at MGM.

I truly am regretful, and must say so at this stage, to appear to carp and complain so much about how us poor scribes are so frequently ignored and abandoned. Most of the time we're briskly appreciated. But there isn't a single biography of a leading writer, at least that I have read, that lacks at least a couple of unforgettable blows to the creative solar plexus.

So. For this *C.H.I.P.S.* (California Highway Patrol) episode, with the eager participation of the show's staff writers, Paul and I created a story in which a couple of unscrupulous members of a political protest demonstration plan to provoke violence in order to be sure of their cause being exposed on the 6 o'clock news.

The genial and tender-hearted star Erik Estrada, that week, was exceptionally outraged by cruelty to children. So this aspect was added to our well-formed story, with the result that each important theme was reduced and diluted, therefore not receiving the full exposure it merited.

How these things linger and twinge ... Erik, could you not have waited a week or so and had an entire show deservedly dedicated to your laudable concern?

Ribbentrop and Dave

A break from celluloid and tape, to tell of a foray into Brit-legit, launched from Hollywood.

A moment's - inspiration? - flash of memory? - what? - and I suddenly wanted to write a stage play about Eric Portman And All That That Entails - 'All' encompassing his sweeping anti-Semitism and driving homosexuality.

The play (fiction) was set in Portman's London theatre dressing room, 1950-ish. He crosses sparking swords with a Jewish film producer, and learns that his young lover has been killed by the Mau Mau (but blame the Jews) in Kenya.

An early reader re-titled it 'All About Grieve'.

Need I add, without arrogance I trust, that amidst all the angst, these backstage folk were, when appropriate, somewhat witty?

Shedding the best light on its roster of London rejections, I could, with some reason, maintain that the open both-sides discussion of anti-Semitism scared even those producers who otherwise appreciated the writing and construction.

Marc Sinden, years having passed, became the script's intuitive editor and firm, persistent advocate. But this very English play, born in California, could not make it home.

More years pass. I read in the *Los Angeles Times* of an English-oriented play running at the Rude Guerilla Theatre Company in Santa Ana. I wrote to the leading spirit, Dave Barton, who expressed interest in and then enthusiasm for what had become *Dinner With Ribbentrop*.

His theatre seated less than a hundred. Each one of the audience, that first night, was miraculously attuned to *DWR*. The first line got the first laugh. Every development, poignant or risible, prejudiced or generous, played out for them with force and accuracy, to needle-sharp response.

One day, still, perhaps, London? Meanwhile, to vary

the *Casablanca* line:

"I'll always have Santa Ana."

Friends

I mentioned having three Hollywood friends: to Milton and Tony, add Ben Brady.

I met him to pitch a 'Movie of the Week' idea. Our amity with Ben and Estelle flourished, until both died.

Ben pleased his father by becoming a major lawyer, then pleased himself by becoming a writer and producer (at all three major networks in turn). His legal background a clear plus, he promoted and produced *Perry Mason* (five years). En route - shows with Dinah Shore and Red Skelton, the latter at first timorous about TV. Ben didn't argue. He simply took Red to a New York café. People gathered round, warmly.

"They like me," muttered Red, near tears, his actor's constant fear dissolved. So he did the show.

I'm told that, periodically, during *Perry Mason*'s run in England, bets were placed on the Stock Exchange that 'this week' Mason would lose a case.

No such tarnishing of the imperturbable lawyer

occurred, nor (Ben assured me) was there the smallest possibility that it ever would.

For me - of omnipotent heroes there are a-plenty. Let's have the occasional moment when a lead character, by sheer accident or good intention misfiring, errs, as humans do. (Memorably: young Dr Kildare *did* lose a lawsuit and paid for it, implicitly, for the rest of his career.)

Ben recruited me for some of his speculations: a lawyer who practises both in London and Los Angeles - a Western version of *Jane Eyre* - and a most ambitious bid to co-star John Wayne and Clint Eastwood. He more than tinkered with a spate of ideas right up to his death, in his 90s, and was determinedly up to date with 'Perry Mason On Line'.

Pick up on John Wayne - cause of the only truly chilling iconic Hollywood experience that ever befell me.

At the premiere of *The Cowboys* (in which son Steve appeared as Charlie Schwartz), The Duke strode massively and rapidly into the theatre, passing a middle-aged man of apparent sanity who literally reeled, giddily (I use the word literally here, with due care) and staring, fetched up against a wall, weak of limb, and whispered:

"I've seen him ... I've seen him ..."

Friends in Hollywood ...

Last word from Robert Young: star for 40 years, committed Christian in a scientific sect, and given to meditation at the beginning of each working day. The only thing he ever told me he hated was semi-colons. But he added:

"In Hollywood there are no friends. Only periodically useful acquaintances."

Why is This Week Different from All Other Weeks?

Reaching back to my young reporting days for a slick phrase, I am reliably informed that some series' actors never read entire scripts. They learn only their own lines. Don't they miss knowing what the stories are? Poolside at the Montecito Apartment Hotel, I asked a grizzled character-actor to tell me the story of the show he'd just been signed to do.

"What story?" he asked. "It's a Western."

Anonymity is also gladly offered to the star who observed:

"Everybody on the unit's talking about this week's script. Maybe I'd better read it."

Hollywood Flashback

She was my school's most beautiful girl. Crisp, fragrant, budding, constantly courted, and my first helpless departure from the pimply Hudisian self-imposed vow to avoid dangerous entanglements.

Nothing happened. But, of course, I went through all the fiery torments, daydreams, suppressed carnality and aggressive purity, without so much as loosening my school tie.

We'd been in California more than 30 years when I received a letter she'd sent to Barbara Windsor to forward on to me.

It was modest, touching, do-you-remember-me stuff, and told me she had five daughters.

(Title of one of my U.N.C.L.E. shows? "The Five Daughters Affair.")

Of course I replied, hoping, truly, that we might meet again on my next trip to London.

Her sister responded: she never read my letter. She'd died suddenly.

Sex in Very Small Helpings

In Hollywood, one woman fantasized urgently to me about what a perfect creative and sexual couple we would make. She didn't exactly say, "I'll have the ideas and you do the writing", but she was close. But if she had, and ever devoted to the punchline no matter what, I fear I might have responded:

"I'll do the work and you have the orgasm."

This is reminiscent of how I described a "collaboration", back in England, which didn't work out: "I wrote it and he read it."

Another: a doctor's aide, hearing that Rita was in Europe, asked me how long she'd be away.

"Three weeks," I informed her.

"Not enough time," she tutted and turned away in

search of other vulnerable quarry.

Honesty, and residual astonishment, compel me to reveal that, at the time, I was on a trolley, fully prepared for an intimate medical procedure which, to my simple mind, took something of the implied romance out of this moment.

T.H.E. Limit

I attended a meeting for a new series, *T.H.E. Cat*, at Paramount. Premise: a former cat burglar goes straight and uses his special skills to help law enforcement. Nice notion.

Fortuitously, I thought up a storyline there and then which was considered suitable: go away and write it.

Got home. Message from the studio: "Forget it. Since you left the studio, the format has been completely changed."

T.H.E. Cat didn't last. Miaow.

Take Me Back to Dear Old Blighty

This reminiscence rightly belongs, I feel, under 'Hollywood' since it is there that the conditions were set that caused our frequent visits back to England.

US Writers' Guild regulations forbid members to seek employment outside Guild jurisdiction (e.g., and principally, England) while still physically in the United States.

This is why, when under more than tolerable income pressure, I went to England in search of employment, without transgressing against the WGA - the most powerful and, by me, beloved union to which I have ever belonged.

Back in England, I was always sure of a cordial welcome from at least two producers - Ernest Maxin (see the Carry On pages of this book) and Steve Walsh.

Formerly a broadcast news correspondent, Walsh headed up the TV Production Company Consolidated in London when we met. It was partners at first sight, and for him the following were written in England:

* *A Monkey's Tale*. Animated. The creation of Jean-Paul Laguione, who has his own studio in Montpelier. It did well in France (as *Le Chateau des Singes*) and I accepted an overall award for it at Indianapolis.

I wrote the song lyrics for this one. I love this work for

its need for brevity and apt allusion. Also - openly materialistic - write a 12-line hit in, say, a day, and it will earn more for you than a movie that obsessively gobbles months. Someone, using modest limits of calculation, figured that a movie written for the US Guild minimum, earns the writer little less than a labourer's minimum hourly wage.

* *W.L.T.M.* TV sitcom. Steve Walsh's creation. Fun and a little heartache with staff and clients of a dating agency (Would Like To Meet = W.L.T.M.) Scripting was exhilarating, but, essentially, a hard ride. There is still hope at the time of writing. Steve Walsh doesn't yield easily.

* *Rogue and Vagabond.* Full TV treatment of the restlessly colourful life of Steve's grandfather ("an absolute bounder" testified Steve's beloved mother). Some of his story was set in Australia, with one terrifying scene where an audience of grizzled convicts took seriously, and dangerously, dreadful events, concerning them, enacted on a stage.

* *Miss Hargreaves.* Originally started work on this Frank Baker magic-realism story in Hollywood, for

Mort Abrahams and Al Uzielli. In time, it passed to Steve Walsh and I went to England to work further on it. It's currently awaiting its fate at the well-known oasis, Hope Springs.

In one draft, Miss H poured forth a poetic searing evocation of a wartime romance, in the 1940 London of nightly air-raids. It owed everything to my girl of that time, who, when we met post-war, after she had undergone punishing hardship in Czechoslovakia, asked me:

"Do you still think I'm attractive?"

These lines are unlikely to be included in any filmed version of the story ("unless greatly reduced, Norman, because people don't go to the cinema to listen to poetry"). But this book, so far, is my only chance to try to see to it that this palpitant, still hurting verse is not lost entirely:

INCIDENT IN THE KING'S ROAD

Soon we might fall, as twisted as the steel
Mingled with rubble in this beloved wasted street,
Maimed, as if Death, not satisfied with our destruction,

Wanted us ugly and repulsive at our end, where
Minutes before, we were beautiful and young.
So we urged each other, in mutual plea,
To defy the fall of bomb with the thrust of life
Even as the Chelsea scena heaved about us
And broke and went into flame
And so did we, blazingly encoupled, only once,
Against a crumbling wall,
Lit by guns as pounding as our hearts
And all else comprising us.
Forced by the time to be wiser than our years,
We knew it was enough
That we merged and survived,
Smiling, holding, ever to memorise
Ourselves, young, saying NO to death from the skies.

All right, mes amis. People may not primarily go to
movies to listen to poetry. And David Lean, an
incontestable genius of cinema, declared that what is
seen is more remembered by film audiences than what
is said. All homage to Sir David's aquiline shade, but
ponder, for a patient moment, just a few random

'unremembered' film phrases:

* "I'll have what she's having."

* "If you long for the patter of tiny feet, rent some mice."

* "I'll think about it tomorrow."

* "Frankly, my dear, I don't give a damn."

* "Make my day."

* "I make more money than Calvin Coolidge - put together."

* "Round up the usual suspects."

* "Infamy, infamy! They've all got it in for me!*

* "Is that a gun in your pocket, or are you pleased to see me?*

* "Why wouldn't God have mercy on my soul? It belongs to Him."

* "She sat on my lap. Unfortunately I was standing up at the time."

* "She could make a bishop kick in a plate-glass window."

* "Frankie! Your mother forgives me!"

* "It was Beauty killed the Beast."

* "Elvira, convalescing from pneumonia, tuned in to a

BBC light musical programme, had a fit of hysterics and died of a heart attack."

The last is from a dialogue-driven movie directed by David Lean, Coward's *Blithe Spirit*.

Resume Walsh: screenplay of my stage play *Henry and Margaret*. Re. live theatre production of this Henry VI drama (told from the French point of view), one legit company warned that it takes them nine months to decide on a submission.

Okay, provided that, if and when production draws frenzied first-night cries for "Author!", Rita doesn't have to go on stage carrying a cremation urn.

Favourite lines - if only to prove that a comedy writer, even in tragical-historical Shakespearean mood, never rests: Henry's servant, addressing his horny young master at bedtime, says:

"Flights of angels sing thee to thy rest."

Henry: "They'll have their work cut out tonight."

Don Quixote Strikes Back, stemming from a deeply imaginative script by Finnish director Paivi Hartzell: this is among the 2 or 3 unproduced projects I regret most of all. Aside from the usual obstacles, its chances were reduced to virtually zero, by the solid opposition of Spanish interests to any version of the classic other than its original.

The King and Me

The way I heard it, Elvis Presley's managerial genius, Colonel Tom Parker, played golf with an entrepreneur and, on a handshake, agreed on a film for Mr Presley at a $1,000,000 fee plus 10% of the take starting with the first box-office dollar, and a budget not to exceed $1,500,000 (today, this wouldn't buy the script).

The deal merits dissection, and earns an obeisance to Col. Tom for his engaging practicality.

Think of it. Many managers stipulate production budgets commensurate with the status of the stars they represent. This can be a most expensive salve for tender egos: because ...

... any film can flop, with no profit to come. Col. Tom's practical way, abjuring pride in status, virtually assured a great take for Presley. Only God's disapproval of pelvis-wiggling, expressed in city-block-size meteors obliterating all theatres concerned, could prevent

Presley from collecting his original million, plus a tidy tithe of the profit virtually certain to accumulate from the box-office returns of such a low-budget production, with such star power.

The Colonel was no less shrewd in image presentation. I asked him what we could best do, no matter what plot twists, to ensure that our star always generated sympathy.

"Kid," said Col. Tom, "have him pat a dog."

Presley's time was limited, so it was a case of make the film virtually immediately. A script was quickly acquired. It 'needed work'. I was hired at my biggest fee yet.

It certainly needed work. It was about a secret agent. I blame no one because the error was shared: and this was that it should have been abundantly clear that this was not ideal casting for Elvis Presley, any more than a rock-and-roll singer would immediately impress as perfect for Sean Connery.

Someone, in the enthusiasm of the moment, advised that all would be well:

"When writing, think secret agent but write Montana

shepherd."

However, with a profoundly experienced and practical producer, Arthur Nadel, in full contribution, I set to work.

Arthur's cool warning was couched in vivid terms:

"Why am I the only one who knows the house is on fire?"

And burned to the ground. Our script, helplessly sophisticated, predictably failed.

Prompt action was sensibly taken. A suitable Western script was acquired (or had been waiting in the wings) and thus, to my regret, my chance of association with the most spectacular popular-music phenomenon of the twentieth century vanished in a puff of gunsmoke.

The company, National General, nevertheless generously gave me two tickets to the Academy Awards. Very acceptable. But this was the year of two assassinations and, out of respect, the ceremony had to do without a stage show.

A disaster of an assignment, rewarded with admission to a tragically truncated Awards event. There is, Heaven alone knows, a fitness to things.

As we entered the theatre, Rita, more than ever stunning in a new gown, was approached by an autograph hunter:

"Are you anybody?"

"My dear," said Rita, "who isn't?"

The Urge to Produce

Trailing the constant Hollywood-bound procession of The Young, The Beautiful, The Hopeful - and the doomed downsides of all these categories who pour into town to be discovered and rewarded - there is a less numerous but steady stream of sane, successful businessmen aiming To Become Movie Producers.

One such, William Thompson, a refreshing personality, acquired a script or story called *Daughter of Bonnie and Clyde*. He was partnered by an Englishman, John Levingston, of some flair and charisma, who built his own automobile and dubbed it a Straightley because it clearly wasn't a Bentley.

This was all real fun. I was given almost a free hand and concocted a storyline which, however, could not quite disguise its explanation, at the end, that it was all the inner ravings of a distorted mind.

Other than that, all I can summon from the memory-mists is the matter of The Book Of The Film.

Bill Thompson wanted to revel in everything to do with film-making, and to see The Book Of His Film in print was high up on his list. Thus, months before any possibility of the film being made, he got a paperback written and printed. So, somewhere in a vault, the one and only paperback edition of *Daughter of Bonnie and Clyde* waits patiently.

Now: why do such warm, balanced provenly likeable and practical men as Mr Thompson get drawn to a business so remote in style and spirit from their own? Try this:

Eager to embrace his thrilling new milieu whole-heartedly, Bill adopted some of the current ShowBiz sloganry. And thus he exclaimed with open enjoyment, over and over again, such then popular Biz clichés as "I'm excited!" and "This'll blow their minds!" This might explain why he turned to film-making: because these two phrases, I submit, he rarely had the chance to utter with zest during the practice of his original occupation - undertaking.

Soap Without Hope

My first visit to New York lasted ten fleeting, blissful days, housed at the Parker Meridien Hotel on W 57th Street - Carnegie Hall one side, Russian Tea Room the other. Purpose: meetings with Henry Slesar, effortlessly inventive all-round writer who was in the process of putting together sample scripts for his new soap-opera formula: 5-part serial stories every week, Monday to Friday, under the heading of *Mystery Street*, introduced by a Welles-like anchorman.

I came up with a sinister tale of rich degenerates, burdened with a dissolute unmarriageable son, all leading to murder. I called it 'Garden of Evil' - and it was no surprise that the prolific Henry had, years before, published a dissimilar tale with the same title.

We conferred on the story and I wrote an Outline, in New York, for inclusion in the package to be presented to the network.

Prospect, collaboration and location were all perfect = much too good to last.

Location: the warm saying about Americans (they all have two hometowns - their own and London), amended very simply in my case - birthplace London cannot be replaced in my heart. She engages my steady and irreducible love; New York quickens my pulse.

Aside from an invigorating professional compatibility with Henry, another indissoluble link was soon forged between us. We both carried in our wallets wrinkled lest-we-forget newsprint photographs of that small Jewish boy - big cap, warm overcoat, fragile little knees, hands up under brave German guns - in Warsaw, on his uncomprehending way to death.

All went well with *Mystery Street* until a recurring Biz doubt surfaced: would viewers tune in to different casts each week, even if introduced for a few sonorous moments by a familiar personality? How could there be any semblance of show-loyalty without recurring Familiar Faces?

But fear not. A solution was put forward by GKW (God Knows Who) - that courageous individual who steps in when Things Go Wrong. His suggestion: tell the same stories we had already prepared - through the active involvement, each week, of a family of mystery writers. They'd hook the viewers, for sure, and honour would be satisfied.

Say nothing of the immediate additional regular-cast costs. Consider only that we would end up with an unwieldy concept - a project that was neither a cosy, compact series nor an adventurous, roving repertory.

Henry met, by chance, the brilliant TV programmer Brandon Tartikoff, in a network corridor, seized the moment and, as they walked, asked for reconsideration of the solution. He got it, in four strides: immediate cancellation of the project.

The late Mr Tartikoff can scarcely be blamed for writing off, there and then, a troublesome project, more likely to compound its problems than resolve them.

Differences

Halfway across the world, on my first flight to LA, I scribbled: "Comedy series idea: differences between English and American conduct and attitude."

I can't speak for other English writers, but my guess is

that many have spawned the same notion over the years and the Atlantic. There was one series so based - *Dick and the Duchess*, starring Hazel Court, of my J. Arthur Rank days. But the format hasn't been tried lately. Perhaps the time still isn't ripe. And maybe it never will be. Because, a patient, charming MGM executive, having heard my pitch, put me on track decisively:

"Please understand that to your average American, allowing for exceptions, there is only the American way. So, for instance, a thumbtack can never be a drawing pin and trying to draw humour out of such differences chokes in a fog of polite bewilderment. And get this: your Ted Heath band was popular here, via record sales. All publicity to the contrary failed to shift US fans' conviction that this was an American band."

Regretfully, I had to add that a film I'd seen on TV as an American movie classic was actually made at Pinewood Studios.

In short: comparisons with the English way of doing things would far more likely produce bewilderment than comedy.

"So don't bother, Norm."

Mums and Dads

Almost before we'd recovered from jet lag, we gave Pollyjack a holiday to America. Nothing other than seeing us again could have induced my mother to board an aeroplane where she held on to Jack's hand for the entire 12-hour flight.

We gave them a good time - and so did Boris Ingster when I took them to Culver City's most celebrated acreage. He provided a car to whisk them round the MGM lot, where they saw the Andy Hardy house 'neverything. Memorable though this was, to tell back in Wembley, I think - I quietly observed him - Jack was most impressed, to rare and brief tears, to be able to reach up in our garden and pluck an orange from a sheltering tree.

Polly enjoyed it all - most especially seeing the grandchildren - but never felt at ease in a country where the police visibly carried guns. She didn't live long enough to see, in the age of terror, some of Britain's cops issued with firearms.

That was the last time I saw my father. He succumbed to - what else? - heart. I went to England for the funeral. Then my mother finally fell ill and I got back in time to see that she couldn't identify me.

Rita's lively, divorced mother, Ethel, known as Robbie, had a holiday, together with her sister, Greta, and they embraced California with gusto. When she left, Greta, with pride, wanted to express her appreciation, but frankly told us that she could not afford to take us out to dinner or lunch. So she presented us, from the Farmers Market, with an enormous Polish ham. We named him Stanislaus. Later, she sent us a hand-embroidered Irish linen tablecloth big enough to make a tent. The ham plus cloth costs would have covered a more than adequate meal for ten people in a restaurant, but restaurant spelled extravagance to practical, spunky Greta.

And Rita held her mother's hand at the last moments, in her beloved native Achill, County Mayo.

One more Dad (if not Mum-and-Dad) story, begs inclusion.

My agents, literary ones remember, once employed an English girl. After a while, she asked if she could introduce them to her parents. Rather an odd request, they thought - but, okay.

Came the moment.

Enter Harold Pinter.

Well I'll Be Fugued

Hollywood lives or commits hara-kiri on its ability to anticipate, and sometimes create, public taste. So it's a grave concern, always, to determine: what's 'in' and what's 'so last century'.

Item: someone who knew my love of baroque conscientiously called me at 6 a.m., so that I should not appear to be 'out of it' in early morning encounters, to let me know, breathlessly:

"Bach is out. Too repetitive."

I was unhappy for Johann Sebastian, but comforted that at least he escaped ageism in his time, or he would have been unemployable during his final 25 years. ("Y'see, Jo - no one over 40 can write a Passion.")

Indian-ese

It's time to record that, correctly claiming ignorance, I wisely declined an offer to try to write a script about

American Indians. I found myself regretting that, somehow, I was not really at ease writing dialogue like: "White man fuck with forked prick."

On a Swiss Roll

I set forth from Hollywood to pursue work, in animation, in Switzerland and Germany.

In a villa on the hill overlooking a Swiss lake - where else? - a series was hatched which, like oh so many, deserved a better fate.

'Bill Body' was an enthusiastic, optimistic character working for a sports equipment firm who, with his family, became involved in sports-oriented stories. The first fact I learned, along with the team of writers, was that the most popular sport on Earth was (and maybe still is) table tennis.

I wasn't too enthusiastic about the offer, with the result that the oldest negotiating put-off in The Biz backfired on me. Offered seven scripts, I got my agent to ask for, if not an unprecedented fee, certainly a hefty one. I might have known: it was agreed immediately.

The creator (sorry - one of the few names I can't

summon) wanted to make the series in Hollywood, with local producers. I recommended the veteran team of Arthur Alsberg and Don Nelson, so prolific a pairing that, though not under contract there, they had an office at Hanna Barbera's North Hollywood studios where they were currently working on *The Jetsons*.

Arthur and I flew to Switzerland and he was rapturously received by the creator, the writers and the genial, firm Story Editor, Australian Joan Ambrose. Also involved was Tibor Mezaros, who ran an animation unit in Kecsemet, Hungary, where production would be completed.

The episode of mine I remember with some sentiment, was 'Butterhooves', about a plodding Clydesdale-type horse, sneered at by sleek racing and show-jumping steeds for his clumsiness. Finally, of course, he triumphs by rescuing, through his great strength and patience, some trapped people.

With childish pride, I have to report that, when the stint was over, NH, the world's worst-organized traveller, managed to cross the lake, get on a train and make it to Paris to meet Steve Walsh. There, equally characteristically, I couldn't find the hotel, located within a stone's throw of the Arc de Triomphe.

There are so many stories about cynical Hungarians - but consider adding this one. I tried to explain the meaning of the word 'scoop' to Tibor, thus: if only one newspaper printed a certain story, what would you call it?

Tibor shrugged, smiled, resigned:

"A lie."

How and Why to Whoosh

Through Steve Walsh, I became Story Editor on the animated series *Waldo*, creation, from his books, of writer-illustrator Hans Ludwig, of Connecticut.

My first contribution to this Cologne-based venture resulted from what I learned about the structure of half-hour animation episodes during two seasons' work on development at the masters of the style, Hanna Barbera:

Get to the point - fast.

Commercials catered to, you have about 27 minutes story time for a 'half-hour' show; leisurely setting-up cuts into time that can otherwise be used in the sacred cause of getting on with it.

"Whoosh!" I said, to illustrate this essential tactic. And 'Whoosh' became the phrase of the year when discussing *Waldo* ideas. Like: "The stolen chart is in that big dark house, guarded by whoever. Whoosh! - let's go get it, even though there's a snowstorm and a forest fire."

Waldo (not to be confused with an identically named character elsewhere) was a big white dog, gifted with speech, a pacific and loving credo, and a good deal of magic with which to conquer time and space. He was accompanied by a mouse, Zelda, who had screeching, tone-deaf ambitions to be a soprano, and, of course, Michael, a questing boy - "Waldo, tell me about ..." - which the dog was always able to do, patiently, dismissing violence and anger with:

"Michael, there's always another way."

The dear fluffy creature was expert in the gentle martial art of Aikido when limited physical action was absolutely unavoidable.

We prepared the scripts in Cologne, where the series

was also physically produced. Thirteen episodes were shot and shown on Cologne TV.

Recalled with some pride: an episode of mine where a company of captive animals, awaiting vivisection, made a break for freedom, singing appropriate new words to Beethoven's 'Ode To Joy'. And Zelda, reduced even further in size, once entered a computer's complex innards to deal with an especially evil virus.

Cologne Cartoon's boss, Ege Egenolf, presided massively over the project. We were given a charming apartment where, nightly, we gaped at German TV and discovered that the local version of America's *Wheel of Fortune* game show was considered, in Germany, to be a 30-minute commercial because of the prizes offered.

One Sunday off, Rita and I walked along the Rhine's bank, noting, en route to the twin-spires Cathedral, the chalked letters 'KKK' on the bridge structure. We found a row of thronged restaurants where we had a lunch vast enough to energize an entire troop of Valkyrie on a Valhalla-bound vault through fiery clouds.

While we ate I mentioned that my cousin, Sergeant

Pilot David Cohen, was shot down over Cologne during the RAF's first 1000-bomber raid. As I said so, a musician ambled by, playing, on a plaintive flute, Israel's 'Hava Nagila' ('Let Us Rejoice').

Characterization

Not that I'm often asked to advise would-be writers but, in the matter of characterization, in Hollywood I have come across one very brief phrase that should always be fundamentally consulted. It was given to Garson Kanin by a veteran New York police officer:

"All men are pricks and all women are crazy."

Amend, modify, render subtle, present crudely, vary as you must, in comedy or drama - but this is the key.

Why Go Under?

Not just a dry ageist time in Hollywood; this one was arid.

But a fortuitous Australian Film Festival, in LA, provided, on Rita's astute suggestion, an extremely welcome alleviation of the drought.

A phone call got me put through to the wrong Mr

Williams (Brian) who, in the event, turned out to be the right one - Executive Director of the Queensland Film Corporation. He leapt at my suggestion that I might be useful in running a Writers' Workshop in Brisbane.

Pine- and Holly-wood experience, coupled with the magic invocation of the Carry Ons, and I was on a Quantas flight in no time.

Seventeen hours later, I was as far from Stepney and Hollywood as I've ever been. Brian did it in style: gave me a hotel apartment, overlooking the Botanical Gardens.

On its doorstep, a few days later, a hotel pageboy did a brief tap dance for me, hoping to be discovered and, from the land of Ned Kelly, flown to a new life in California as the Aussie Gene of the same name.

And so I settled into the hardest work I've ever done in my writing life (dead heat with these pages).

Seven writers, seven scripts - morning and afternoon individual sessions, plus preparing a detailed diary for the Corporation's records. When Rita came out for two weeks, she imposed a three-day rest.

Reward: out of the seven projects, two achieved

production. Comparison is patently very shaky, mathematically speaking, but that's a much higher average than the wastage statistics at major studios. Hope becomes history in astonishing numbers in Pine- and Hollywood, as projects are, horrible term, aborted.

My one comment on the Australian social scene: on the way in from the airport, the first Brisbane sign I saw, identifying an organization, was that of the Rechabites. They, as I recall, advocate temperance.

Comment: they face a daunting mission in Australia.

And: ever alert for bigotry, I nevertheless deduced, quickly, that only the dimming of the letter 'T' on a restaurant neon sign, naming the dish of the day, accounted for the offer of 'Baked Rabbi'.

And Finally
The World According to Me

In *Harlequinade*, Terence Rattigan neatly caught the aberration of people in The Biz being essentially out of touch with life beyond stage or studio. An actor, trying to recall when he last played a provincial town, cannot name the year but did remember, vaguely, that electricity was in short, flickering supply, the trams weren't running and there were no reviews, indeed no newspapers ...

Patiently, the stage manager prompts:

"You don't, by any chance, mean 1926 - the General Strike?"

Yes I am in and of The Biz. But I have, nevertheless, in mood ranging from exasperation to agony, been aware of the real world and its endless, terrifying turmoil.

And ...?

I believe that there could be clean water, abundant food, ample living space, full medical care, clean air, an intact Arctic, mutual acceptance of cultural diversity, education, and the whole range of moral you-name-its within a measurable time frame, without a single army unit involved; and enough resources left over to send a cosmopolitan crew, Australians to Zulus, to Jupiter if that enterprise is felt to be absolutely necessary.

Possible, aye - if the human race can rid itself of its inhumanity.

If it can't, then I, for one, don't see how it can - no, I

won't flog the obvious phrase to death, but will merely say - 'continue'.

Universal Revisited

I check in with a cop I don't know. Nearby - a seated line of burly men.

Says the cop to me: "You here to try out for 'King Kong'?"

Ultimates

The Most Beautiful Woman I have ever met:

Rita Hayworth. She lived up to Orson Welles' comparisons:

"Horses sweat. People perspire. Rita glows."

Most Handsome Man:

Tyrone Power. Linda Christian's gaze at him, confirmed.

They were visiting Eric Portman backstage in London.

Best advice about The Biz:

"Talent is all very well. Then you have to use your head" - Sammy Glick in Budd Schulberg's deathless

Hollywood novel, *What Makes Sammy Run?* It must be obvious by now that only by rare accident did I benefit from this advice.

Two theatrical legends at breakfast:

Lynn Fontanne: "At the end of Act Two, I'm going to pause and smile quizzically at the audience before I exit."

Alfred Lunt: "Lovely idea, but the play closed last night."

Lynn: "What's that got to do with it?"

Maestro in Class:

Cello Pupil: "Sir, in this passage I want to express all the fear and urgency implicit in the piece. What shall I do?"

Piatigorsky: "Play faster."

To the point:

Stewart Granger: "You lucky bastard. You can act."

Eric Portman: "You're luckier. You don't have to."

NH According to PM

Paul Mason, remember, hired me to script a movie, which was finally titled *The Hong Kong Wink*.

It opened with the hero, released from jail, slaking his pent-up sex at his favourite brothel, and going on to seek revenge against whoever had had him unjustly imprisoned.

"If it were me," I told Paul, "I'd get my revenge first and then get fucked."

"That, Norman," said Paul. "Is the story of your life."

Norman Hudis

Norman Hudis, born 1922 started as a junior reporter and joined the RAF in the Second World War. Towards the end of his five-and-a-half years' service, he was on the editorial staff of the Cairo-based Air Force News and travelling, as the war's youngest war correspondent, the length and breadth of the Middle East .Post-war, aiming to become a playwright, he had a modest success with his first effort, *Here Is The News* – enough for Pinewood Studios to offer him a screenwriting contract. Then he went freelance as a prolific writer of B movies. Hudis-scripted, low-budget *The Tommy Steele Story* was a million-pound box-office success and Hudis was then offered a long-term contract by its producer Peter Rogers. With director Gerald Thomas at the helm, the Carry On production trio was complete, for the three of them went on to film Carry On Sergeant and five others, including the archetypal Carry On Nurse – top British box-office film of its year. Not so incidentally, Hudis is married to SRN Rita. They have two sons, Stephen and Kevin.

Following the huge Carry On success, he moved to America in response to offers. There, he has written for The Man From U.N.C.L.E., Marcus Welby, Simon and Simon, Baretta (Mystery Writers of America Edgar Allan Poe Award), The Story of Esther (three awards), Hawaii Five-O, Cannon, etc. Hudis now works for producers in both countries.